THE GREATEST MOM EVER!

TERRI CAMP

Loyal Publishing
www.loyalpublishing.com

I'm going to be THE GREATEST MOM EVER!...even if it kills me.

TERRI CAMP

Loyal Publishing, Inc.
P.O. Box 1892, Sisters, OR 97759
www.loyalpublishing.com

ISBN 1-929125-08-9

00 01 02 03 04 05 06 / 7 6 5 4 3 2 1

To Shileen (long i, long e, no r)
I love you with my whole heart!

Contents

Acknowledgments

This book was a cooperative effort. My role in the creation of this book was minimal. But since the names of all the people who have helped me will not fit on the front cover with mine, I must thank them here.

First, I would like to thank Jesus who is the author of my life. He created my passion and orchestrated the fulfillment of my dreams.

To my husband Steve, who played mommy all those nights when I disappeared to my computer, I can't even begin to express my thanks to you, but I have a lifetime with you to try. And don't forget—I saw you first! And I love you more!

To all of my children, Ashley (13), Christi (12), Cathy (10), David (8), John (7), Briana (5), Erica (3), and Bryan (2), I never knew how easy it would be to love so many. I have truly been blessed!

Shileen Groth, I just know you're gonna cry when you see this for the first time. When we were little, we didn't want to share our toys, and here we are all grown up and sharing our joys. This book would not have happened if it weren't for you. Thanks for making me hysterical.

To Mom, I want to thank you for having more faith in me than I did in myself. Without you, I would not be.

Dad, you taught me that the only boundaries in my dreams were the ones I placed there myself. Thanks for believing in me.

To Mike Farris, a guy who was "not really" as he seemed, and Chris Jeub, who together ganged up on me and pushed me over the edge and sent me spiraling—upward toward my dream.

Jeff and BJ, thanks for giving my dream a name.

Lori Tibbits, you did a great job helping to make my dream even better! It was indeed a pleasure to work with you.

To my Great Times mommies. This book is for you!

Matt, you can drop my dreams anytime, as long as your wife picks up after you.

THE GREATEST MOM EVER

When I envision The Greatest Mom Ever, I do *not* see myself in the picture anywhere. I see a tall woman with a long dress, hair up in a bun, and a flowing cape tied around her neck. She is usually preparing a marvelous meal for thirty dinner guests, with a smile on her face and a song on her lips. She has a spotless house, and even a dog that is obedient to her kind way of speaking. Her children all dress in white and never seem to have a hair out of place. Her husband always greets her with a dozen long-stemmed red roses and sweeps her off her feet.

She somehow manages to find many hours to spend helping those in need. She also spends a great deal of time in prayer and Bible reading every morning before her first child has crawled out of bed. She exhibits a Christlike attitude, from dawn till dusk, even when no one is looking.

The only part of this picture I even closely resemble is wearing the flowing cape. I once played Batman as a young child and would tie a bath towel around my neck and go through the house yelling, *"Nana-nana-nana-nana—Batman!"* My sister and I even tied a washcloth around our dog and called him Batdog.

Even though the memory is rather charming, it doesn't entitle me to claim myself as The Greatest Mom Ever. Even though I pretended to be Batman as a child, I am still hesitant to venture into our attic where there are real bats. I suppose that alone would disqualify me from wearing The Greatest Mom Ever cape.

If what I envision is true, then I will *never* even come close to The Greatest Mom Ever title. However, in spite of all my shortcomings (and yes, I am short), I serve a God of miracles. He has this marvelous ability of taking the ordinary and turning it into the extraordinary. I serve a God who can take a short, dark-haired, nothing of a woman, and empower her to be what *He* has envisioned as The Greatest Mom Ever.

He has taught me through all the Mommy Moments, the Treasure Moments, and the God

Moments that to be "great" you must become "the least of all." It is when I humble myself and say, "Okay, God, whatever You say," it is then He gives me a "to die for" heart. When I die to my selfish desires and dreams, I find peace in His presence, knowing that I am walking in His will. It's not about how great I can be—it's about letting Him be great through me.

If we surrender all to God, trusting in Him, then we cannot go in the wrong direction. Be encouraged by His promise: "Trust in the Lord with all your heart, and lean not on your own understanding; in all your ways acknowledge Him, and He shall direct your paths" (Proverbs 3:5-6). If we are in prayer and doing what He requests of us, He will enable us to follow through.

Look to Jesus. He will show you how to surrender if you are willing to walk in His footsteps. Jesus was God in the form of man, yet He humbled Himself by dying on a cross for a lost world that didn't deserve His grace. On the eve of His death, He sought no "special" treatment. Instead He washed His disciples' dirty, smelly feet. Why? Love. Sacrifice. Commitment. His entire life was one of humility and service to those weaker than He. He sought no praise. He sought no glory. He only sought to follow His Father, even if it meant He would have to die to accomplish the Father's will.

Dying to self is the key to being the best mom you can be. When you surrender all your hurts and frustrations, your wants and desires, His desires will become your desires. He will give you the strength and the joy to pray and to live, "Not my will, but Thine be done!"

Part

MOMMY
MOMENTS

One

1

YOU DESERVE A BREAK TODAY

Today was one of those days. You know, you awaken to children fighting over how many English muffins a four-year-old can have. The big problem is, he's fighting with a two-year-old. The conversation begins innocently enough. The four-year-old wants another one, and the two-year-old obviously thinks he has had quite enough.

"You can't," says the two-year-old.

"Yes, I can!" shouts the four-year-old.

"NO!"

"YES!"

"NO!"

I pray, "Lord, just don't let them wake the baby who was up three times last night." Too late. I add a quick plea, "Lord, help me to be kind to these children who have somehow taken me from blissful sleep into a tremendous wrath." Not really praying, but speaking to the Lord, I ask, "Where have I gone wrong lately?"

Sigh. I suppose these things wouldn't happen to The Greatest Mom Ever. Or maybe they just wouldn't bother her. But I have days like this and, frankly, I find myself in need of a break now and then. Nothing fancy, just a little time away to renew and refresh both body and spirit. I suppose it's different for everybody, but for me it's a nice deep bubble bath: a quiet, uninterrupted, long hot soak.

The only problem is that my children haven't quite figured all this out. I just get nice and cozy—then there's the knock.

"Who is it?" Silence…another knock.

"Who is it?" Silence…another knock.

"What do you want?"

"I'm bleeding." Cathy announced.

The rule is: When Mom is taking a bath, you may not disturb her unless you are BLEEDING! However, the child standing outside my bathroom door did not sound like she was BLEEDING! She was simply *bleeding*.

"What do you want me to do?" I asked. "Do you want me to get out of the tub and hand you a Band-Aid under the door?"

"No, it's not that bad."

"Then why are you telling me?" I inquired.

"You told us to come when we are bleeding." She ever so innocently replied.

It finally dawned on me why most moms take showers. It's not because they waste less water or because they feel cleaner. It's so they don't hear anything like, "Mom, I'm bleeding!"

I reiterated the rule; "You may not disturb Mom unless you are BLEEDING. Are you BLEEDING?"

"No… Good-bye."

Another knock on the door.

"Yeeessss?"

"It's Christi."

"What do you want?"

"I want to come in and show you something," she stated.

"What is it?" I said, getting a wee bit upset about another interruption.

"Can't I just come in and show you what Daddy found outside?" she pleaded.

"Is it a snake?" I said hesitantly.

"No, it's not a snake, but it's really neat, too," she said sounding almost like if it *had* been a snake that would have been even better.

"Are you sure it's not a snake?"

"No, Mom, it's not a snake. Can I come in? Pleeeaaase!"

I, being the wonderful life-experiencing mom that I am, relented and granted her favor with the queen. (I mean, allowed her to come in.) I got out of the nice, warm tub and unlocked the door, then returned to my refuge full of bubbles.

She entered the bathroom with a very large *toad*. "I wonder what it would think of bubbles?" she playfully asked while dangling it over the tub.

Suddenly, there was a great multitude in the bathroom. All of the children had heard of the great discovery and had come to see the giant toad for themselves. There I was sitting in a bathtub, with wonderful, glorious bubbles, a room full of children, one daddy, and a toad hopping all over my towel.

I looked at Steve with a look that said, "This would be a good time to read my mind."

Steve, being the great mind reader that he is, said, "Okay, kids, Mom has seen enough. Let's go outside and see what the cats think of the toad."

They all left, but my towel had been slimed.

Other duties must be done in the bathroom that require some time and privacy—both of which seem to run short in our house. Once such duty is…reading. Most families' central meeting place is the kitchen. Our family is different. For some reason our family tends to congregate in the bathroom. If I want to use the bathroom to…uh hmmm…read, I must dismiss the crowd that has followed me.

Briana followed me in one morning thinking it would be okay for her to stay if she simply said, "Close eyes." She then placed one hand over her left eye and one hand sort of over her right eye. She was really peeking. It was quite cute, but unacceptable.

When John was around three months old, time to "read" in the bathroom had been virtually eliminated. If I couldn't take care of business, it didn't get taken care of. That particular day, I had put John down for a nap and went into my bathroom. I locked my bedroom door and my bathroom door.

I was just getting to the interesting part of the magazine when I heard Ashley yell, "Mom, David's *bleeding!*"

He had fallen trying to climb on the stepstool to go potty "all by himself." I had to take him to the doctor to get stitches in his chin.

The next day, I went to my bathroom to finish that article from the day before. I had barely found my place to begin reading again when I heard Ashley yell, "Mom, David cut himself. He's *bleeding* all over the house."

My immediate thought was, *How bad could it be? Maybe I'll just stay here.* Then my thoughts drifted back to the day before, and I realized I could not remain in the bathroom to finish the article. I closed the magazine and tossed it into the trash on the way out the door.

David was standing in the living room with blood dripping from his hand. From the looks of it, I thought he had cut off his finger. It's amazing how much blood can come from a little two-year-old's finger.

Back to the doctor for more stitches. As I was going through the "drill" of telling the doctor how this all happened, I finally broke down and cried, "I know. I'm a rotten mother—and I will never try to go to the bathroom again."

Moving from California to Iowa made it even harder to get private bathroom time. I can no longer escape behind several sets of locked doors to use the bathroom—well, not in winter unless I want to brave the subzero temperature of our master bathroom. It could just as well be an outhouse. It is so cold. I think Steve has opted not to insulate better so I don't read too much and accumulate more unnecessary doctor bills.

But here is my real secret to personal renewal. When taking a bath, turn the water on as hot as it will go. Pour in a generous amount of Avon Aromatherapy. (This is not a commercial for Avon. It just works for me.) Then turn the water off when you have depleted your water heater, and cold water is coming out.

Approach the water cautiously as some child may have turned the knob to cold while you were not looking. (There is more than one reason to never leave a young child alone in a bathroom with the water running.) Turn on a teaching tape of some kind. Sit back, put on a purple mud mask, relax for at least thirty minutes, and then get out refreshed. You will then be calm and serene.

Until you look in the mirror after you have just received a package from the UPS man and realize you forgot to wash off the lovely purple mud mask.

2

SPRING CLEANING

Some people make New Year's resolutions. Not me—I make "New Baby" resolutions. I always become a "clean fanatic" the last six weeks before I have a baby. I get out the toothbrush and clean all the little crevices in the kitchen floor. I go out on the roof and scrub the bird doo-doos off. I even move the refrigerator and the piano two days in a row because they have probably gotten a little dusty since the day before. Over the last thirteen years my "nesting" instinct has kicked into full gear each time before I am about to have a baby, enabling me to do some extraordinary cleaning that I would not have done otherwise.

Not only do I want to clean my house; I want to reorganize my life. If my life were in order, I would probably want to reorganize someone else's life. I rework my schedule and try to figure out how to get everything done in a given day and still be alive to tell about it. Then I begin implementing my new schedule, only to find out I have forgotten to leave time for me to go to the bathroom.

When it comes to reorganizing the house, I am always amazed at what we have collected since the last time I was "nesting." What does one do with thirty-one stocking caps, seventy-five gloves (notice that is an odd number), fifteen pairs of snow pants, twenty boots, thirty-five coats, and one hundred and forty-five pairs of socks?

One of our Christmas traditions has been to give the children socks in their stockings. Perhaps this year I will give them a box to put their socks in.

If I knew then what I know now, I don't think I would have ever gone "garage-sailing." I never would have set foot in a Wal-Mart or Target store. I would have never uttered the words, "That's neat" to anyone in the position of giving me things. I am a slave to my things.

I must constantly clean, move, pick up (especially with a two-year-old around) and be frustrated with the constant state of counters, bookshelves, closets, and drawers.

I recently read *Clutter's Last Stand* by Don Aslett. He is a little more fanatical than I am when it comes to cleaning; however, he definitely inspired me to cut the clutter and to dejunk the bunk.

I decided to have a trial run and practice dejunking at my mother's house. She and I chose to tackle her bedroom and her clothes first. She had piles of clothes. She works at a J.C. Penney outlet store, so she can get some really good deals on things. The problem is she never gets rid of the clothes that were a good deal five, ten, or fifteen years ago. She finally realized she had too much. For the most part I couldn't help because I had to hold the baby, but I offered to fulfill the strategic role of cheerleader.

She would hold something up and say, "I like this, but…"

As soon as she said, "but…" that was my clue. "Throw it out! Throw it out! Yeah, Mom!" I would cheer.

She ended up with seven big garbage bags full of clothes to give away. It was amazing to see the change in her attitude from first going into her room to the final bag being taken to her van. I was inspired. I felt like going home and getting rid of *everything* I owned!

I drove home and began dejunking in my bathroom. I thought, *That will be the easiest room in the house to dejunk. How much stuff could two people have in a bathroom anyway?* Rusty razors and ten-year-old perfume samples look a lot less useful when you are "nesting" rather than when you are just a mom who needs to use the bathroom in two minutes or less.

Eeek! Why do we have three half-used bars of soap? I don't even like bars of soap. We have a liquid dispenser. Out with the soap! I cheered myself on as I tossed the soap into the trashcan.

"What are you doing?" my husband questioned in unbelief. "Those are perfectly good bars of soap."

I guess I better postpone dejunking until my husband isn't home, I thought. But since I had so much momentum going, I hated to stop. I explained my mission to him, and once he understood my motivated madness, he gave me nearly full authority to dejunk—as long as I left his stuff alone.

After the bathroom...my closet...no, too emotional. I'll do the boys' room. Where is the boys' room? I know I got them one of those cute rugs so they could play cars in an imaginary construction site. Where is it? First I'll have to plow through all the toys to find it. But I don't feel like plowing, I feel like dejunking.

I called in the boys. "Clean this room. You have one hour."

I was obviously in no mood to play games with them. After a half-hour, I noticed they had made absolutely no progress.

"Okay, boys, you have a half-hour more, *anything* on the floor in a half-hour will be confiscated."

A half-hour later it looked the same. I was armed with my giant garbage bag ready to throw away everything they owned. Then I realized how over-whelming the task must have seemed to them. I had mercy or grace. I'm not sure which.

Anyway, I got the broom and swept everything into a big pile in the middle of the floor. I put every-thing away in their room into the right bins. Then I dumped out just the farm animals.

I called in John, "Everything you can pick up in five minutes stays. The rest goes to the attic until you can learn how to pick these things up on a regular basis."

He didn't do very well. He rummaged through trying to find his favorite things. After five minutes I went in and noticed he had about ten animals. Steve promptly carried the rest to the attic.

I knew John would not sneak up to the attic to get that favorite horse. But, he did pick up those ten animals every time I asked him to after that.

Leaving just a few things in the bins was a quick way to dejunk—except I put everything else in the attic. (I don't think that counts.) Bats live in the attic, so I left the attic dejunking to Steve.

So much for resolutions. Are there any cheer-leaders out there, who would like to come over and shout, "Throw it out! Throw it out! Yeah, TERRI!"? You'd have to hold the baby though.

Chapter 3

DINNER'S IN THE FREEZER

Several years ago when I was still in the "honey-moon" stage of cooking, we had Thanksgiving meal with all the relatives at our house. (The "honeymoon" stage is when you want everything to be really gourmet and perfect. The smallest failure can result in tears.) It was my opportunity to shine for my in-laws.

We planned to barbecue the turkey. (You do that kind of thing in California in November.) However, when Steve went to light up the grill, we were out of briquettes. All was not lost, though, because after a quick trip to the store, we were ready to get cooking. The turkey cooked a lot faster than I expected, so it ended up being done long before the "enchanted broccoli forest." Even though my timing was not perfect and some dishes were served cold, I was so proud of our barbecued turkey. It was cooked to perfection.

Steve was pleased that we could have Thanksgiving at our house because that meant lots of leftovers. Steve's dad carved the beautiful bird. He put the remainder of the carcass that still had some meat on it in the refrigerator. We had heard that the meat would stay moist if left on the carcass.

After several days, Steve commented that it would be nice to have a turkey sandwich. "Oh yeah, we have turkey in the fridge," I replied. I filed that information in my brain to be retrieved at a later date, like the next day.

After a couple more days passed, I noticed this…uh…smell coming from the refrigerator. Being a couple of months pregnant, I made a mad dash to the bathroom. My mind began to race. *What do I do? Would Steve mind if I called him to come home from work for this? No, probably not a good idea…The garbage man doesn't come for a few more days, and I can't leave that smelly thing in the garbage can. I must take action—now!*

I opened the refrigerator and as fast as I could, I pulled the neatly wrapped carcass out. Without breathing, I ran to the garage, put the turkey down, then ran back into the house and took a deep breath.

Now what do I do?

A brilliant idea popped into my head. *I will put it into another garbage.* (I think that's against the law now.)

I opened the garage door and ran the carcass out to the car. *Oh no! I don't want that in my car.* I put it on the hood. *That'll work!*

I got in the car and began to drive. I kept looking behind me. I was sure I would be found out. *Nope, no dogs chasing me yet.*

I found a dumpster, heaved it in, and ran back to the car. *Whew! I made it.* Driving back to the house I felt like I had somehow participated in a great feat of espionage. I should have worn a dark coat on my adventure.

Since my little carcass incident, I have made a Thanksgiving motto. As soon as the turkey is carved I say, "Out with the carcass!" I have learned since then that it is okay to take all of the turkey off the bone. It is even okay to freeze it. I just cut up all the leftover turkey into bite-sized pieces and fill up Ziploc freezer bags with about two cups of meat in each bag. Of course, you should label and date the bags so you don't forget what is in them or forget how old the meat is. (I only tell you this because I forget to label everything.)

Have you ever noticed that almost all frozen food looks the same? Corn looks like pumpkin. Pumpkin looks like chicken broth. That really gross bean stuff that no one liked looks like beef stew that everyone loved. Since I never label anything, we sometimes end up eating that really gross bean stuff a couple of days in a row. For some reason, I never learn my lesson. When I fill up a Ziploc bag with a meal or leftovers, I always presume I will know exactly what it is in six months.

I used to try cooking thirty meals at a time; but most of the things I made, my family didn't really like. I would make five meals of the really gross bean stuff and then they would have to eat the same bad meal five times.

One time I made spaghetti sauce for twenty meals. It seemed like a great timesaving idea, except that I burned the spaghetti sauce and instead of throwing it out, I used it anyway. Every dish that I put the spaghetti sauce in tasted disgusting.

After making the family suffer through about two meals, I ended up giving all the spaghetti sauce meals to a friend for her pigs. She told me the pigs devoured the cannelloni. A few months later she gave us one of the butchered pigs as a gift. We joked, "Who needs Iowa corn-fed beef when you can have California, cannelloni-fed pork?" They were, by the way, the best pork chops I have ever had.

Another time I attempted to make a large batch of spaghetti sauce, it turned out perfectly. As I was putting the bags into the freezer, one of them began to fall. I caught the bag upside down and spaghetti sauce oozed down the front of my body, filled my left shoe, ran down to the floor, into the freezer, and under the freezer. It was late at night. (Do you think I would actually try this with my children up? They would want to "help.")

The freezer was splashed with red, and I was exhausted. I quickly closed the freezer, hoping it would just go away. "Out of sight, out of mind." I called in the dogs from outside. They licked and licked and licked. When Jake lifted his nose from the floor and looked at me thankfully, I thought, *I should have put a bib on him.* I think you can still see traces of spaghetti sauce in the freezer.

After all these mishaps, I changed my ways. Dinner is a breeze now. I set aside one day a month. (This may sound like I'm really organized, but I'm not. I just pick a day and do it.) I buy twenty-four pounds of ground beef, four roasts, and six chickens. I put the roasts in my very large Crockpot™. I begin to simmer the chickens and brown the ground beef. This is the greatest way I have found to cook.[1] After the items are done, I freeze meal-sized quantities in bags. When it's time to cook dinner, I take out the meat I need, put it in the microwave for seven to eight minutes, then add it to whatever else I've made. I now can have a meal ready within twenty minutes.

I have long since left the honeymoon stage when it comes to cooking. I have now advanced to the "just-be-thankful-you're-getting-fed" stage. My motto has become, "Better is a dinner of herbs where there is love than a fattened calf with hatred" (Proverbs 15:17).

NOTES

1. I got the idea for cooking all the meat ahead of time from the cookbook *Base Cooking*. You can order the cookbook by writing to Donna Zito, P.O Box 14, Glenwood, IA 51534.

Chapter 4

ON MY
SOAP BOX

When I dream of mountains, I picture myself twirling around in a meadow on top of a high mountain in the middle of the Alps singing at the top of my lungs, "Climb Every Mountain!" The view is incredible. I can see for miles. The air is crisp and clean. Even the mud looks clean from the top of the mountain.

But since I'm not Julie Andrews and I do live in Iowa, the only mountains I get to envision on a daily basis are stinky, dirty, dingy piles of clothing that never seem to go away. As I look at my mountains of laundry I'm not even tempted to twirl around and gleefully sing "Climb Every Mountain."

Instead I sing a song that goes like this:

This is the pile that never ends. It just goes on and on my friends. Some people started doing it not knowing what it was, and they'll continue doing it forever just because this is the pile that never ends. It just goes on and on my friends...

I figure that if I keep singing loudly enough, my children just might think I have gone absolutely mad and might banish me from the "Mount Neverest" room forever.

I'm going to let you in on a little secret. I have a sleeping bag that has been in my laundry room for at least a year. It's waiting for space in the washer—when there is nothing that "needs" to be done. But just when I'm getting close to being done, the inevitable happens—someone gets sick. Before you know it, three more kids are sick. In one day a family of sick children can produce more laundry than an entire regiment of soldiers. Why is it that two-year-olds turn their heads *away* from the bucket? Oh, but that is another topic.

One *big* advantage to home schooling is that if there isn't any clean laundry, the kids *can* wear their pajamas and no one notices. One morning I had not yet made it out of my pajamas, but I drove Ashley over to feed her horses anyway. It was one of those Mommy Moments for me. My daughter looked at me and said, "Only you, Mom!" It was the moment I had longed for all my motherhood—the moment my daughter would roll her eyes and realize that she did indeed have a complete kook for a mom.

As much as I try, the children insist that I am not a kook, but a cook. I have tried on numerous occasions to inform them that I have indeed now gone stark raving *mad*. But, they don't buy it. They still come to me and say, "What's for dinner?"

After days of endless laundry, I will often tell them that they are getting nothing for dinner that has the slightest chance that someone will spill it, drip it, drop it, or wipe it. That pretty much narrows the choices down quite considerably. "Let's see…hmmm…you can have dry cereal!"

To which, of course, they all shout, "Hurray!"

One of my mommy-ponders is how is it possible for an eighteen-month-old to manage to get oatmeal in his socks? I have also tried to figure out why I never have any clean towels. We have about twenty-five dishtowels. But, we *never* have one in the drawer. Where do they go? Do washing machines really have hidden digestive systems?

Another mommy-ponder of mine is, if clothes touch the floor, does that mean they are dirty? My children are more than willing to pick a spoon up off the floor and use it. They are willing to drop an apple outside on the ground, wipe it off on their shirt, and eat the apple. But, if they have a shirt that is on the floor, they will not pick it up and wear it. This doesn't make sense to me.

I've decided to create a new line of laundry products. I think the soap will be a big hit. I'll call it "Mountain Moments." My slogan for the television commercials (starring my eight darling children, of course) will be,

Do you have a Mount Neverest? Try "Mountain Moments," and you'll be glad you did. From the moment you open the box, it will spread an aroma throughout your laundry room that will even make the potty scent from the wet sheets pleasant and inviting. Do you smell mildew coming from the towels left in a clump? "Mountain Moments" will turn them into snow-capped mountains. Relax and enjoy your Mount Neverest again!

When I was a little girl I remember Mom declaring, "Laundry Day!" We would gather all the clothes from the hampers. We only had two kids and two grown-ups, but there sure was a huge pile of clothes. We'd pile all the dirty clothes at the top of the stairs and try, without actually picking them up, to get them down to the basement. Often my sister and I would sit on top of the huge pile and ride it down like an avalanche. The only problem was that on occasion I would find that I had stuck my hand right on someone's underwear. "Oooh—skidmarks!" I'd scream. I hated carrying all that laundry down to the basement.

My mom had no system for laundry really. She was just basically doing crisis management. We would finally get all the clothes down to the basement, and then we would have to sort them all. I kind of thought it made them dirtier sitting on the cold basement floor.

I was so happy when I discovered bins. I use huge Rubbermaid containers to transport, sort, and deliver all of our laundry. I only have four because that's how many will fit in the laundry room. (You can tell a house that has been designed by a man because he puts the washer and dryer in a little, tiny space)

Our previous home was brand new with five bedrooms, a gigantic master bath, and a laundry room that was only six feet by six feet and tucked as far away from the bedrooms as possible. In fact, you had to go through the little, teeny-tiny laundry room to enter the house from the garage. There wasn't even a sink in it! There was one cupboard above the washer and dryer (like any normal-sized person would be able to reach inside the cupboard). I had to locate a stepstool every time I needed to get the Bounce sheets out.

And what about the names of soap? Who comes up with these names?

"Okay, everyone up! We're going to wash 'All' the laundry today."

"What do you mean? Aww, Mom."

"'Cheer' up. It could be worse. You could be poor and not have any clothes. You could not have electricity and have to wash your clothes in the 'Surf.' Consider it pure 'Joy.' Stem the 'Tide' of this poor behavior and make your attitude become white as 'Ivory Snow.'"

Laundry is one of a home schooling mom's biggest challenges. It's one of those things that you think you get a handle on, then suddenly, the bins are full again.

Take Jill for example. One day, she had all her laundry done. She was feeling pretty good about it, too. She had delegated, as a good home schooling mom should. Nathan folded all the clothes. Heather, being the "observant one," thought it a bit odd that Nathan was folding clothes that didn't look quite that clean. When she questioned him, Nathan just said the clothes were stained.

Well, the next day as Jill was putting the clothes into the drawers she noticed a "smell." *Hmmm?* she thought to herself. *These clothes aren't clean.* It became obvious to her when she saw food, dirt, juice, and other stains on the clothes. *Well, so much for those clean clothes.* She gathered the rest of the "clean" laundry and took the clothes back to the laundry room. *So much for a job completed,* she thought as she erased the checkmark next to "laundry" on her chart.

Life continued on as usual for Jill until she and the kids dropped by their local library for a visit.

Nathan climbed out of the van and headed t
door. When Jill caught sight of his pants, she was
horrified! His pants were not just a little dirty. They
were disgustingly dirty. He had grass stains down
the entire length of his pants. Trying not to lose her
temper in front of all the clean-looking people who
were walking into the library, she asked impatiently
in a hushed voice, "Nathan, why are you wearing
those dirty pants?"

"Uhhh, I thought they were just stained, Mom."

To be quite honest, I think having a child wear
clothes he thinks are stained might be a lot better
than the three-year-old who simply cannot decide
what to wear.

He rises early and puts on an outfit. Shortly after
breakfast, finding he has dribbled a bit of milk on his
shirt, he confidently marches back to his room to
find a new shirt. But, of course, the blue pants don't
go with that striped shirt. He remembers that he has
some checked pants that would look simply marvelous. He shuffles through the first drawer, pulling
some out so he can get a better look. *Not in there*, he
decides. He then weeds through the clothes in the
second drawer. *Nope, not in there either.* Perhaps, he
will find them in the third. He digs some more and
then notices, *Oh, there they are.* He picks the pants up
off the floor and puts them on.

Being a helpful little tyke, he grabs the rest of the
clothes on the floor and stuffs them back into the
first drawer.

He goes out to his mother who takes one look at him. She obviously doesn't know how much looking he did to find those checked pants, and she tells him to find his red overalls. Back to the room the little tyke goes. *Red pants, red pants, must find red pants.*

He doesn't know the color red yet, but he's sure he's found them. So he puts them on. By this time, the poor little tyke is so tired he just leaves the heap of clothes on the floor.

When he finds his mother (in the laundry room, of course) he tells her he's dressed. She just looks at him and shakes her head. *He found the red overalls. But how in the world did he manage to put them on backwards?*

As his mother makes her way down the hall to a bedroom to put away (what else, clothes) she sees out of the corner of her eye what used to be a clean room. She calls the little boy in to pick up his room. (For some reason, this mother leaves the child to complete this task on his own.) When she returns, she is satisfied.

A few days pass and we find mother, once again, in the laundry room. She is sorting clothes and finds, *folded pajamas!* She becomes suspicious and realizes that three-fourths of the laundry belongs to one little boy.

Just as she's beginning to feel a screaming attack come over her, her precious son comes in and says, "How do I look, Mom? Aren't I handsome?"

He's wearing his three-piece suit that she just bought him to be the ring bearer for Aunt Josephine's wedding next Saturday. He managed to get the pants on the right way. His little clip-on tie is straight and perfect. His hair is slicked down and parted. And chocolate ice cream is dripping off his chin...

Chapter 5

LOSING IT!

I have found that it is a whole lot easier for me to show perfect strangers the love of God than my own family members. Oh, how I long for my children to see God's perfect love in me every minute. But I must admit there have been days when I've wanted to send my kids to Grandma's house. And then never pick them up.

There are some Mommy Moments when I ask myself, *Will I ever regain my sanity? Or am I "losing it"? Is my mental functioning completely gone, or will it someday resurface without my even knowing it?*

I'm sure there are many days when my children wonder, *What has happened to our mom?*

This is what a mother does who has lost her mind. (I'm sure you will not recognize yourself in the following scenario.)

You have been busy cleaning bathrooms all morning because your mother-in-law is coming for a visit the following day. The children are playing quietly, as they have been instructed. You realize lunch should be well underway. As you walk to the kitchen, you pass by your green children...*Green children!* You stop dead in your tracks as your brain tries to figure out *who* or *what* has invaded your dining room. There on the floor, looking up at you, smiling like angels, are two of your not-so-angelic children. *Well*, you reason, *that's not so bad. At least I can scrub them and make their green skin a little less vibrant.*

Your calm reasoning begins to crumble quickly when you look just beyond the little leprechauns. You realize they have not only marked on themselves, but they have also marked on the wall. Huge circles of green permanent marker decorate the dining room wall. Your mind has left the thought of lunch. It has left the thought of cleaning the bathroom. It has even forgotten that you spent a great deal of time and pain bringing forth these children.

Suddenly, without warning, you forget that you have a sane mind. You forget that your mother-in-law will not really think you are a rotten mother. You forget that the invention of wallpaper was for this very purpose. You just forget everything.

You begin scrubbing and scrubbing and scrubbing. You scream at the two, really adorable children, *"Get out of here!!"* Under your breath you murmur things like, *I'm never letting markers into my home again...I'm never letting children in my home again.*

After you realize there is absolutely nothing you can do with the walls, you decide those children must have a bath. As you near the bathroom you hear water running. You ask yourself, *I wonder who is running bath water?* When you open the bathroom door another "angel" is smiling up at you. He has decided to be helpful and fill the tub with water. The problem is—he *forgot* how to turn off the water! As water spills over the edge of the tub, you feel the heat in your face rising as you scream a second time, *"Get out of here NOW!"* You throw a towel down on the floor and try to soak up the water, but the carpet is soaked. You begin murmuring something about hating carpet in bathrooms, vowing to yourself— *never again, never again.*

This is the moment you realize your mind has gone. You desperately need to find it, so what do you do?

You could be really spiritual and get out your Bible and look up those passages dealing with anger. You could look heavenward and say, "Help!" and mean it. You could call your husband and say, "How many children were here when you left this morning...And are you going to be counting when you get home tonight?"

When you think you are going insane, just tell yourself over and over, "For God has not given us a spirit of fear, but of power, and of love and of a sound mind" (2 Timothy 1:7). Remind yourself that you were indeed given a sound mind by your Creator. Maybe that will keep you from doing something "really" stupid when you're staring at a green child.

The next time one of your children dumps the salt shaker out in the living room, has diarrhea twelve times, washes herself with chocolate milk, empties your purse, or messes up someone's art project, you can have a sound mind. Believe me, I know. Erica did all those things—today.

Look to God. Seek Him morning, noon, and night. Keep looking to Him for guidance throughout the day. Especially take the time to give your day to Him. In the morning, before you even look at your day planner, look to God and say, "This is Your day! I will rejoice and be glad in whatever comes my way."

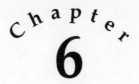

Chapter 6

BEAUTY IS PASSING...

So just what exactly does the Greatest Mom Ever *look* like? How does she fix her hair? How much makeup is "acceptable"? Does she *have* to wear dresses?

Some of my friends say it is wrong for a woman to cut her hair. Other friends tell me it is wrong for a woman to braid her hair. Other friends say a woman must cover her hair. I know people who believe women should dress plainly, wear no makeup, and avoid stylish haircuts. Some godly women I know wouldn't even think of wearing a pair of pants. Then, some of the godliest women I know live in jeans.

How can this be?

I have tried, unsuccessfully, to figure out what a Christian woman should look like. I have always desired for people to recognize that I was a Christian even if they saw me from across the street.

How does a Christian look anyway? As I tried to figure out what other Christian women were wearing, I came to the conclusion that all good Christian women wore skirts. So I began only wearing skirts. Not long after, I discovered that some Christian women wore pants. *Oh good*, I thought. *Now I can wear pants and still be a good Christian.*

Then I joined the ranks of home schoolers. Everyone knows that all good Christian home schoolers, especially those with a lot of children, wear (all together now) *jumpers!* Just the other day I was joking with some other home schoolers about what we would wear to the NICHE (Network of Iowa Christian Home Educators') convention. "Jumpers, the required uniform, of course" was their response.

I felt like I was finally getting my act together. To "appear" to be a godly Christian woman, I must wear jumpers. So I bought jumpers. I could even buy them from Sam's Club. "Hey, this is cool. I can look godly and still be fashionable," I mused. There was only one hitch.

Every time I looked in the mirror, I looked *fat*! Not only that, I looked short! Okay, so I am short.

There is no other way for me to look, but I'm really not that *fat*! So, in my quest to "appear" godly, I purchased several jumpers and didn't feel godly at all wearing them—just round.

So then I reasoned that it's not buying the jumpers that's godly—it's making the jumpers. That's the step I missed. You have to *make* your own jumpers in order to truly be godly. Everyone knows that all godly home schooling mothers with lots of children make their own jumpers, *denim* jumpers.

Now I was excited about this. I felt the Lord's hand on this project. I knew this was what I had been searching for. I made my jumper. It was so cute, but I still did not look godly—only *fat*!

Argh! I began to wonder if when I got older and started developing (fat cells) would I stop worrying about how I looked? I did not want to be obsessed with my appearance for the rest of my life.

Since I didn't have time to waste in front of a mirror and since I didn't want to draw attention to myself anyway, I decided what God really wanted was for me to wear jumpers, and He didn't want me to fix my hair, wear makeup or jewelry. I thought I had it all figured out.

Then the McKims came, a family of 15.

Guess what? They wear makeup, fix their hair, and they don't wear jumpers. And, believe it or not, they are godly people, too.

Back to the beginning. *(Sigh.)*

Now what do I do? I asked myself as I looked in the mirror. *I'll ask Julie McKim.*

I told Julie about my struggle, and she gave me what I thought to be very wise advice. She told me to dress how my husband would want me to dress. *That will solve my problem,* I thought. *I'm sure he will give me the answers I need. He will spell it out for me. He will go through my closet and throw away all the clothing he doesn't like or doesn't want me to wear.*

So, I approached my dear husband and said, "Honey, how would you like me to dress?"

He looked me up and down and said, "Without clothes."

His glib remark did not help at all. I don't think it would be very godly for me to walk around without clothes on.

After some more prodding he was even less helpful. He simply said, "You look fine."

I was wearing sweats at the time.

So, I'm back to the beginning again.

If I can ever get this clothing thing settled, then I can work on the makeup issue. Makeup wasn't an issue for me when I was younger. I had nearly perfect skin and didn't need makeup to look just fine.

I began to wonder, though, when people started asking me if I had had a rough night. "You look tired," they'd say. I wasn't really tired; I just *looked* tired.

I began once again to look in the mirror. Every time I would look in the mirror, I would quietly say, *"Yuck!"* I don't think most people would see me and say, *"Yuck!"* But I felt "yucky" as I looked at my overweight body. The reflection that stared back at me was not smiling—it was sagging.

I was blaming the "yuck" feeling on having to tuck in my stomach, rather than my shirt. When I looked in the mirror, I did not see "godliness."

Since I hadn't progressed very far by following my husband's input, making my own jumpers, or even asking other people's advice, I decided to go to the Source. As I sought His wisdom, a verse continued to go through my mind, "Charm is deceitful, beauty is passing: but a woman who fears the Lord, she shall be praised" (Proverbs 31:30). It was there that I found the answer to my struggle.

I realized for the first time what God wants me to wear. God doesn't look at me through the same kind of mirror I do. God doesn't look at my outside! He looks straight into my heart. I couldn't get past the way I looked on the outside to see how I looked on the inside. What I needed was a day at the health spa for my spirit. I needed to spend more time on my innards and less time on my "outards." We can't look "godly" enough if our spirit is "yuck." We can dress the part. We can wear the right makeup or no makeup. We can buy jumpers, make jumpers, or wear sweats, and it doesn't make one bit of difference to God.

I have decided that when I look in the mirror as I'm talking to myself (I always talk to myself while looking in the mirror, don't you?), instead of asking myself how I look, I'm going to ask God how I look.

Then, I'm going to pray, "Lord, make me pure in heart as I go about my day. Cause people to see You in me. If I go out, I want to glorify You. But if I stay home, cause even these precious little souls to see You."

As I think about it, the children I have been entrusted with see me at my worst. They see me with my p.j.'s on. They see me shortly after giving birth. They see me on days that I was up most of the night with sick children. They have never once complained to me that I look "YUCK!"

In fact, one day as I was sitting at my computer typing away, my son John, who had been allowed at one point in his life to watch *Sleeping Beauty*, came up to me and said, "Mom?"

"Yes, John?" I replied.

"YOU are the fairest of them all."

THE MIRROR

I look into my mirror
and wonder what You see.
Do You see godliness
deep inside of me?
Or do You see someone
who just cares about her hair?
Do You see a person
who doesn't really care?
Do You see the extra
pounds of fat?
Or, do You really
care about that?
Do You see a person
who has a holy fear,

For a precious Savior
that she holds so very dear?
Do You see a person
whose heart is pure?
Do You see a person
who knows You, for sure?
As I look in my mirror
help me to see,
The kind of person
You want me to be.

Chapter 7

PHASES

I'm entering a new phase in my life. I did not expect to enter this phase while still so young. I figured many more years would pass before this phase would begin. But alas, I am right smack dab in the middle of it. No amount of kicking and screaming will turn the clock back now.

No, I'm not referring to the new mommy phase, the two-year-old phase, the rebellion phase, or even the menopause phase, but the "my-child-doesn't-think-I'm-perfect-anymore" phase.

You think you've entered the *Twilight Zone* when one day your sweet little twelve-year-old innocently approaches you and says, "I don't think I'm going to raise my children like you have." Or perhaps she says, "When I'm a mom, my children are *never* going to misbehave in public." Or my favorite, "When I have children, my house will be immaculate!"

This precise scenario happened just the other day. "When I'm a mom," Ashley began, "I am not going to spank my children. I'm going to use other forms of discipline."

She then stated, "My house will be clean— *always*. I have my schedule all worked out." She proceeded to tell me her minute-by-minute itinerary that described how she was going to run her family of thirteen children and eight hundred German shepherds.

She consoled me by saying, "Mom, you can hide out at my house anytime if you care to see how to run a house efficiently."

I could hardly contain myself. She had such a matter-of-fact opinion of the world. She had all the answers and none of the current problems. Ashley reminded me so much of myself when I was her age. I felt like I was travelling back in time.

I decided it was time to tell Ashley a little story.

Once upon a time, a young mom had two small children. One was named Ashley, the other named Christi. I had been sick for weeks because I was pregnant with Cathy at the time. One morning I awoke feeling GREAT! so I decided to tackle cleaning the house.

I began at 7:00 A.M. by mopping the kitchen floor. At 7:30 A.M. the girls got up. I fixed their breakfast and proceeded to vacuum the living room. In the kitchen I could hear the girls giggling, and then I heard a CRASH. I ran into the kitchen only to find that Ashley had decided it would be fun to dump her sopping bowl of Cheerios onto the floor. Christi, seeing how much fun that was, decided to fling her bowl of milky Cheerios across the room, too.

I cleaned up the girls and sent them off while I remopped the floor.

Another CRASH! Christi was standing in the living room holding a leaf from a plant, which had been sitting on the mantle. It was one of those spider plants with the shoots that hang down. She apparently had tried using the plant as a rope. The worst part was, she was giggling as she looked at the smashed pot and dirt all over the fireplace hearth and carpet. Dirt was everywhere.

After revacuuming the living room, I proceeded to clean the bathroom. The bathtub hadn't been cleaned for quite some time. When I finished the tub, I realized the girls were not around. I looked out the window and could not see them. I began to panic. I ran around the house, then outside. They weren't out front, and they weren't out back. I yelled and yelled.

Then I heard, "Here we are, Mom!"

There they were in a corner near the house, sitting in a hole they had dug in the sand. (We lived in the desert at the time.)

"I'm giving Christi a bath," Ashley laughed as she dumped a bucket full of sand on Christi's head. Christi and Ashley were both covered from head-to-toe in sand.

To the *clean* bathtub they went, tracking sand through the kitchen, through the living room, and into the bathroom.

After I took them out of the bathtub, I collapsed in the chair. *When will this day be over?* I thought. I glanced at the clock. It was only 9:00 A.M.

After I told Ashley this story, she said, "Well, my kids aren't going to make messes."

As I listened to her talk of the future, she was so sure of herself and her circumstances. She had her life all planned out—where she would live, what she would do, and how she would raise her perfect children.

I also had my life planned out, but God had other plans for me. I think about the plans I was so sure of. *My* children were never going to have to do dishes. I was *never* going to spank my children. My children were going to be raised "free." They would not have the restraints that other parents put on their children.

My plans to be a spank-free parent did not last long. The first time I spanked my children, I thought my heart was going to break. I ached for them.

Ashley and Christi had run across the street while I was watering the garden. Across the street from our house was a vacant lot. We also called it the tumbleweed patch. The children were fascinated by the weeds and wanted to get a closer look.

When I told Steve what they had done, he said, "I hope you spanked them."

"Well, no, but I did warn them of the gravity of the situation and why they must *never* cross the street on their own."

"Honey, they could have died if they had been hit by a car while running across the street, and all you did was give them a lecture in words they probably couldn't understand?"

It was the first time Steve was ever appalled at my parenting skills, or lack thereof.

The next day, sure enough, the girls ran across the street while I watered the garden. I had to retrieve them because they weren't trained to come when I called. I marched them into the house and spanked them. They never did cross the street again without permission.

As a young mom I didn't want to give my children boundaries. I thought they should be free to be and to do whatever they wanted as long as it wasn't illegal or it didn't hurt anyone. Fortunately, I learned the error of my thinking fairly early.

I discovered that children need boundaries. They need to be told something is "off-limits," or that certain behaviors are unacceptable.

When I was a child of twelve, I thought I had it all figured out. I saw what I perceived as my parents' failings. I was *not* going to make the same mistakes they did. I laugh when I think about how naive I was back then. There are times now when I begin to think I have "arrived." I start feeling like I do have some answers. I feel more secure in my parenting. I feel good about my relationship with my husband. I start thinking I actually have it all together.

Then…reality sets in. I survey the house and see that perhaps my cleaning schedule hasn't been working as planned. I see children doing their chores with a bad attitude because not only are they going to have to do the dishes, they are going to have to clean the toilet, too! I sometimes wonder if I will ever get this mother-thing figured out.

Perhaps we can learn from our twelve-year-olds. I have learned from some of Ashley's comments. I have learned that a tidy home is important to her. I have learned that I do not always have all the answers and that I always need to be willing to grow and to change. I have learned to listen to her, to encourage her, and to try out some of her ideas. What do I have to lose? If she is right I may end up with a tidier house, and if she is wrong, she may learn how to give more grace.

There is a bright side to this "my-child-doesn't-think-I'm-perfect-anymore" phase. At least, for now,

I *still* have seven children who do think I'm perfect. The other day John even said, " Mom, you're perfect!"

When Bryan is twelve and forces me into the dreaded "my-child-doesn't-think-I'm-perfect-any-more" phase, then, Lord willing, my older girls will have put me into the "my-mom-must-have-been-a-saint" phase.

> Her children rise up and call her blessed. Her husband also, and he praises her. (Proverbs 31:28)

Part

TREASURE MOMENTS

Two

Chapter 8

ROSE SMELLERS

Getting ready for church that morning had not been a pleasant experience. Trying to get eight children and two adults dressed and fed in spite of missing shoes, missing socks, and missing hairbrushes before 8:30 A.M. was not my idea of preparing myself for worship. I was impatient and cranky. When I rushed down the stairs ready to get in the van, *no one* had on shoes. The children were congregating on the front porch pushing and shoving trying to find their other shoe. I ran back upstairs shouting, "Everyone get in the van—shoes or no shoes!" Meanwhile, I found the final two missing shoes. I rushed out the door, jumped in the van, and to make matters worse, forgot to grab my Bible. Now I was *missing* one more thing.

I glanced back at the children and just sighed. Erica still had the remains of cereal on her chin. Briana had oatmeal on her dress. And John's hair was sticking out everywhere. Then I noticed that Briana had her tights on inside out and there was a huge hole down the front of her leg. That was the last straw for me. As Steve sped to church, I began to question why I was even going. I certainly didn't have an attitude of worship.

We arrived at church a couple of minutes late. The mood seemed somber to us. Pastor had already begun to talk at the front, so our motley crew waited in the foyer. One of the ushers whispered to us that a young man from our church had lost his battle with brain cancer. After Pastor finished praying for the family who had lost their son, we walked the long trek down to our second row pew. I didn't seem to care too much that John's hair was sticking up all over his head. His messy hair did not seem like that big of a deal in comparison to losing a son to cancer.

A wave of differing emotions surged through me as the reality of the young man's death sunk in. We began singing "Amazing grace, how sweet the sound, that saved a wretch like me." It was then the tears began to flow. His death seemed tragic to me. But as I sat there, I felt at the same time a joy for him.

Right at that moment he was sitting at the throne of God. As the words "that saved a wretch like me" echoed in my mind, I began to think of all that Jesus did for me so that I too could join Him in heaven one day. I thanked Him for dying for me. As we sang the last verse "When we've been there ten thousand years bright shining as the sun, we've no less days to sing God's praise than when we'd first begun," it dawned on me that in heaven our days will not be numbered as they are now. I only have a limited number of days to spend with each of my children. There are no second chances. I can't go back and relive one special moment that has passed. I can't go back and cherish the mundane moments. I can only treasure the present.

The missing shoes, missing socks, unbrushed hair, and tights on inside out, no longer seemed very important. I welled up with thankfulness that I had eight children who called me "Mommy." Oh, how I wanted to call an "Oreo hug." (An Oreo hug is simply Daddy on one side and Mommy on the other and all our little stuffings in the middle.) Since an Oreo hug at that moment would have caused quite a scene, I just looked at each one of them and asked the Lord to hug each one for me.

"Lord," I prayed, "show me how to enjoy my children in the mundane moments. It's so easy to enjoy them when we are out making snow angels, or snow dogs, or sledding down the hill. But I want to appreciate them when we are desperately trying to match gloves, zip coats, and don hats. I want to be more patient when I hear, 'Mommy, I need to go potty' as soon as the last coat has been zipped, and we are ready to walk out the door. Help me, Lord, not to think of all the work we went through to get dressed, but remind me that at least she didn't go outside in her pants.

"Remind me, Lord, as I'm fixing dinner and Erica is unloading the contents of every cabinet onto the floor that 'this too shall pass.' Help me not to be irritated with her but to enjoy how funny she looks trying to sit in the little red bowl. When I have said, for the 'umpteenth' time, 'Will someone *please* take out the trash?' help me to realize this is not a federal offense.

"Remind me, Lord, to be less concerned with getting somewhere and more concerned with smelling the roses along the way. I want to stop scurrying and begin strolling! I don't want to be a family that rushes through life. I want to be a family of rose smellers, snowball makers, and puddle jumpers."

A few days after the young man had passed away, I helped serve at his funeral. It was one of the most amazing moments I had ever witnessed. The church was packed. Busloads of people came to this man's funeral. He had made a significant impact on those around him. Our church was full of people whom this man had witnessed to in his life, and there they were, being witnesses even to his death.

When the funeral was over and the cleanup was nearing completion, I sat in a chair in the back of the church. I just intended to sit there for a couple of minutes as I admired all the beautiful flowers that graced our church.

Loretta, a dear elderly woman from our church came down and sat beside me. We talked a bit about how lovely the flowers were and how they must smell heavenly. Then we just sat quietly together for a moment. She took my hand and said, "You too can impact those around you like he did." She must have known my thoughts. I was sitting there thinking that if I died would there be anyone whose life was different, better, or saved because I had lived.

If I had known then what I know now, perhaps I would have written down every word Loretta ever spoke to me. A few weeks passed, and I was standing in the kitchen with Loretta once again. We talked about my impending birth and her impending surgery. We parted with a hug and both of us saying, "I will pray for you." That was the last time we saw each other. She went to be with the Lord one day after Bryan was born.

Loretta impacted my life because she was able to stop and smell the roses with me. I pray that as I continue my journey through life that I too will be able to stop and smell the roses with those whom I meet along the way.

9

CARPÉ DIEM

Do you remember your high school class motto? My motto was "Every journey begins with a single step." I've always enjoyed mottoes. Some might say that's one more reason to chalk me up as strange, but that's okay with me.

I had a science teacher in high school who would write a different motto on the blackboard every day. I looked forward to reading his messages. It was kind of like having one of those flip calendars without having to remember to change it every day.

I enjoy making mottoes for our family. Sometimes the motto will be relevant to something we are studying or simply a Bible verse we are working on.

"Go to the ant, thou sluggard" (Proverbs 6:6) is one of my favorite mottoes. Whenever my children seem to be a bit "slow" at their tasks, I will often shout, "Go to the ant (looking them in the eye) thou sluggard!" That is their cue that they are working too slowly.

Of course, my son John's motto is my all-time favorite. We devised this motto when John was two-years old and often needed just a "little" reminding how he was to obey. He would say, "I do everything the first time, every time, without questions, and a smile on my face." And this is what he would think, *And after I say these words, I will do what I am told.* You see, he was still getting away with delaying his obedience until after he said the phrase. At one point I began to wonder if he was delaying on purpose. But he was so cute saying his motto, so I didn't push it. Now four years later, he doesn't need to say his motto anymore.

I have realized our learning motto is "Seize the Moment!" A friend reminded me of a Latin phrase that means the same thing. So, of course, I searched the Net, and sure enough I found the phrase *Carpé diem*! It is now my battle cry.

When a child innocently asks, "Mom, how come cardinals don't fly south for the winter?"

Carpé diem!

When we are making cookies, I hide all the one-cup measuring cups and make the younger kids figure out how to get two and a half cups.

Carpé diem!

When Ashley comes to me and says, "Where's the town of Dillon?"

Carpé diem!

My children have never "studied" maps, yet the older two could navigate me anywhere.

We read a lot of really good books and when my children ask questions about them...

Carpé diem!

There are times when I think, "But, what if I miss something?" Then, I realize that if I have forgotten to teach them something they need to know, they know how to find out.

But, what if the kid just isn't interested in learning about a certain subject? That's when the motto changes from Carpé diem! to "It doesn't have to be fun, but it must be done." We try to make learning enjoyable, but sometimes it is mundane. Multiplication tables must be memorized. Grammar rules must be learned. But I've found they accept the drudgery much more when they know that if it could be fun, Mom would make it that way.

My children enjoy learning when they see knowledge unite with reality. They still must memorize facts, but I try to show them how the facts relate to their world. My greatest textbook is the world around us. God presents us with so many creative ways to learn if we are open to them. It is vital that we allow God to be in charge of our school. I don't ever want to get to the point in educating my children that I think I have all the material I need. If I rely on Him, He makes sure the children are learning all the subjects they need to know.

I'll never forget one day when I was in algebra class; one of the children stood up and asked the teacher, "What do I need to know this for?"

The teacher responded tritely, "You may someday want to be an engineer or a mathematician."

She lost the kid forever when it came to math. I was that kid. I had no intention of becoming an engineer or a mathematician. I just wanted to know how I could use algebra in everyday life. The teacher lost a great opportunity to inspire me (and the rest of the class) to value math. Instead we dragged our heels through 300 more pages of algebraic equations for the rest of the year.

Several times in my life I have had to approach my engineering husband to help me with an algebraic equation that I needed to know for a "real" life application. When I asked him what was apparently a "basic" question, he looked at me like, *And you're home schooling our children?*

The next time one of your children asks, "Why do I need to learn this?" play reveille on a cardboard toilet paper tube (you can find one in your son's bedroom) and yell, "Carpé diem!"

Then proceed to help the child make connections from the classroom to his or her world. If you are really strapped for a "real" life application, point to a nearby four-year-old (you can borrow one of mine if you want) and say, "When you are a parent, a child like this is likely to ask you about this subject."

Children ask all kinds of questions. I try to remember, for the most part, that my battle cry is Carpé diem! But, I also must admit, that after question number sixty-four, I have been known to say, "Okay, everyone hush now!"

I have discovered that some of our best "learning" happens while we are riding in the car. My children have learned to count by fives. They've learned about speed limits and policemen and tickets. They've learned about inertia—no matter what the claims are, you cannot stop instantly.

Steve and I have explained many spiritual truths to our children while riding in the van. I'll never forget the time we had an opportunity to talk to our children about surrendering to the Lord in the area of children.

David asked as we were driving home with our newborn Erica, "How come we have more children than anyone else at church?"

The door was open for us to explain that God called us to let Him be our "family planner." "Well," Steve explained, "some people 'choose' for themselves how many children they will have, but we have decided to let God choose for us. We feel children are a blessing from God—like a gift that He gives us."

One of our older girls, I don't remember now which one, said, "I want ten children."

Another one of our girls said, "I want thirteen."

Then David, our five-year-old son, not to be outdone by his older siblings said, "I want a thousand!"

Cathy then replied, "Then you'll need another wife!"

Try not to look at the questions or comments of your children as an interruption in your day, but just remind yourself, Carpé diem! You never know where a question or an answer may lead.

Some days I feel like I'm in a rut. Instead of staying in the rut, I load the kids in the van and take them for a drive somewhere. Before I know it, "school" is taking place.

I have often wondered how we are to fulfill the commandment of Deuteronomy 6:7 if we fill our children's days with activities and entertainment. In Deuteronomy 6:5 Moses tells God's chosen people to "love the LORD your God with all your heart, with all your soul, and with all your strength." He goes on to tell parents how they are to teach their children to love the Lord:

> You shall teach them [God's commandments] diligently to your children, and shall talk of them when you sit in your house, when you walk by the way, when you lie down, and when you rise up. (Deuteronomy 6:7)

Basically, Moses was telling parents to seize the moment. Take advantage of every opportunity to show and tell your kids of God's love. "When you sit at home…" When do you sit with your children? Dinnertime is a great opportunity for values-sharing. Sitting at a desk watching your children do school-work doesn't count. I would encourage you, if you don't sit down together for meals, start doing it now. I read a survey a couple of months ago that stated children were less likely to take drugs if they have regular meal times with their families. Perhaps that survey result comes from parents obeying Deuteronomy 6:7.

"When you walk by the way…" When was the last time you took a walk with your children? Walking with your children is an excellent way to get some exercise, but it is also a time to enjoy being with each other. There aren't the demands of "home" calling you. There are no dirty dishes on the trail. There is no laundry waiting at the bridge. It is a time to talk and explore.

One day, it was Columbus Day I believe, we decided we *must* go exploring. We called up a few friends and hit the trail. Not far into the walk, one of the parents spotted a snake slithering across the path. We all stopped and stared at the grass where the snake had gone. Christi had gone on ahead but noticed we had all stopped. She came quickly back to see what we were looking at. She spied it. And no quicker did she say, "Snake!" then she had it in her hands. It was a prime opportunity for me to share that snakes are cursed to crawl on their bellies, not look grown mommies in the eye.

Taking walks is not one of my strengths, but I've known many families who go on a walk after lunch everyday without fail. I remember reading about one home schooling family who would take a walk before lunch. Before they left the house, the mom would put the bread in the oven and the soup on the stove. Can you imagine what their house smelled like after coming in from the brisk air?

I think "driving along the way" also counts. Much teaching and learning can be done while driving because you are all trapped together in one small space for awhile. Just don't get too carried away and forget you are driving.

One day Steve and Ashley were coming home from somewhere when they came upon an accident. Ashley was about five at the time. Steve said to her, "Let's pray for them." When he finished praying, Ashley said to him, "But Daddy, you didn't close your eyes."

One of our favorite car games is the "Alphabet" game. We play it a little differently than most people, however. You see we live in Iowa. In Iowa the scenery is quite unique and changes frequently. Sometimes you are driving down the road and there are beans on the right and corn on the left. Sometimes there is corn on the right and beans on the left. Sometimes there is corn on both sides.

There just aren't a lot of signs to play the normal "Alphabet" game, so we have modified the rules. We begin with the letter *a* and choose a category, like cities and states. We then must each come up with a different city or state beginning with the letter *a*. Then we move on to the letter *b*. The neat thing about this game is that if we say a city, often the children will say where it is located. Or they might say, "It's the capital of Turkey." The great thing about this game is you can choose any category you want. I've even caught my kids playing this without being in the car.

"When you lie down…" My own interpretation of this passage is that Mommy must take a nap every day in order to be refreshed to impart spiritual truths to her children. (That is not really the true meaning of that Scripture. I just threw it in to make you laugh.) However, napping does make me a better Mommy because it helps restore the dead brain cells that I used up throughout the morning. At some point I think mommies end up with a finite number of brain cells to use each day. If we don't get a nap, then that amount decreases. Have you ever sat in a chair looking at nothing? It might just be your cue that you need a nap.

One of the best times in our home is bedtime. No matter what the day has been like, we all gather together for prayer and singing. If someone has been a "grouch" all day, it will subside before they go to bed. Who can stay "grouchy" when they are singing praises to the Lord and praying? And the extra kisses from Daddy are just a bonus to top off the day.

A long time ago I found that bedtime was the hardest time of the day for me. I was simply exhausted from the day's demands. I would find myself getting irritated with the children as they were getting into their beds. Steve and I decided that after prayer time he would put them all to bed. When we both put them to bed, I would almost be rushing him out of their rooms. Now he can stay and spend as much time with them as he wants. It's good for the children, and it's good for Daddy, too.

"When you rise up…" This again is another area I struggle in. I don't like to rise up. I like to stay under my sheets where it is warm and cozy. Yet when I make myself rise up before the children, then I can set the tone in the house. I can put some muffins in the oven. I can put some nice music on the stereo. And I can greet each child with a smile, a kiss, and a tickle. The days that we rise singing and laughing together are the days we enjoy the most.

10

IT'S A
CLASSIC

I have found a way for my family and me to enjoy a richer, more fulfilling life. No, it is not filling our stomachs with cheesecake each day—that would only make us fatter, not richer. It is not even about making money—that would only make us richer, not more fulfilled. I am embarking on a course that leads my children to knowledge.

I happened upon the path to a richer, more fulfilling life innocently enough. I had been praying for a change in our schooling. I was feeling like we were missing something. I couldn't quite put my finger on what we were missing, but I knew that for many of our days the goal had simply been to "get our work done." I knew there was more to a rewarding life than simply having the children do their required assignments. I just didn't feel that only doing math, reading, and writing everyday was enough for my kids.

Sure, they were getting the work done and reading some good books. They were also having fun exploring the study of survival. They learned a few things to do in case they ever needed to survive without us. They learned if they ever got lost in a cornfield (and that actually could happen here in Iowa) that they should level the corn to write the word *h-e-l-p*. But still an element was missing. I knew it must be a character flaw of mine, so I prayed, "Lord, what am I neglecting? Please guide me in the way You want me to guide my children."

Well, God always answers prayer. He doesn't always answer in the ways we expect, however. At the beginning of our Christmas "holiday," I logged on to the Internet and found a Charlotte Mason web site.[1]

I consider myself a home schooling mom who doesn't necessarily fit into any of the theoretical molds, but I am fascinated with Mason's ideas on educating children. She advocated teaching many different subjects in small portions throughout the day. The subjects she emphasized were art, classic literature, and nature. She felt those subjects should be a daily part of a student's education, rather than an "afterthought" when they have nothing else to do.

Reading e-mails from other home schoolers, who were implementing some of Mason's ideas, revealed to me that my children's education was lacking a key ingredient. I had failed to impart to my children a love for the classics. Though we had read many books, we had not read many "classics." Though we drew, we had not examined the works of Renoir. Though we wrote, we had not written with the flair that was prevalent many years ago.

I realized this wasn't necessarily a character flaw (That is good news, don't you think?) but perhaps a lack of understanding. Why had I failed in this? Was it because I looked at a book like *Pilgrim's Progress* and thought, *They won't get it?* Or was it that I thought museums were a waste of time? Or perhaps, I didn't feel qualified to teach what I didn't know? I was not exposed to the classics in school.

Many people don't believe teaching or exposing children to Latin or Greek is relevant. Many don't think spending a few hours gazing at great works of art in a museum or even looking at art in a book is important. Many don't care if their children read *Jane Eyre* or *Silas Marner*. I wouldn't have cared. Studying the "great" books and the "great" works of art seemed unnecessary in our home schooling. I thought my children were too young to appreciate such things. I didn't know that classics could be enjoyed at all ages.

As I began to realize the value of studying the classics, I made a firm decision that I would not allow my feelings of inadequacy to get in the way. I desired for my children to love and appreciate the classics.

I knew that my children might not "take" to the classics like a duck to water, so I decided from the beginning to cultivate their tastes at a slow and steady pace. I recently read that a child must taste an unpleasant food fifteen times before it becomes pleasant to his palate. I question this a little because I know I have tasted at least fifteen peas, and I still do not like the little green things.

However, I do love broccoli, and I *hated* it as a child. The mere mention of broccoli would bring me to the point of gagging. All it took was for me to try broccoli covered with cheese. Then, after I found myself enjoying that, I smothered it with butter. Now, all it takes is a little salt.

All this food talk is to say that an appreciation of the classics is an acquired taste. We may have to begin with an appetizer like taking our kids to a ballet such as *The Nutcracker Suite.* Next, we may move on to a meatier course like the art museum. We may detest the paintings of Picasso, but when we study the works of Michelangelo or Raphael, we may find ourselves staring at Picassos. Or we may find that we still detest Picassos.

When I first began reading the King James Version of the Bible, I stumbled over the *thees* and *thous* and all the words that ended with *eth*, but after a time, the words became a part of me. I began to love the Word of God in a way that was not possible with another version.

The same is true with the classics. At first we may stumble over the rich language, but before long, we will begin to think classic thoughts. If we read classic literature that has characters who exhibit moral integrity, who love the Lord, and who believe in His principles, we will begin to think like them.

Have you ever read a Doctor Seuss book to your children? Whenever I do, I go around talking in rhyme. "Tonight we're having spaghetti! Do you think that you can get ready? You'll need to use a plate. Hurry! Hurry! Or you might be late! And don't forget the fork, or tomorrow you'll be eating pork." What you read begins to become a part of who you are.

Our family adventure into the world of the classics had begun! If my children were going to develop a passion for the classics, I decided *I* must be passionate about them. I perused my books on the shelf and looked for a good classic to curl up with on the couch. Many people on the Charlotte Mason loop had talked about reading *Jane Eyre*. I saw the book on my shelf, but I knew nothing about it.

I picked up the book and examined the binding and the worn-looking pages. *I guess someone must have liked the book if it's been around this long,* I thought.

I opened it and began reading about the author Charlotte Bronte, who wrote the book in 1848. I began to think perhaps I had made a mistake choosing this as my first road on my new adventure, but as I read the first few pages, I began to feel myself being transported into her life. I began to read in an English accent. I realized I had been missing out by not having read the book before. With each page that I turned I was further indebted to Charlotte Bronte and to Charlotte Mason for showing me a new richness to life that I had not known before.

I desperately wanted my children to be able to experience the same feelings I was having while reading this great book. My first thought was to begin reading it aloud to them. I decided against that idea because the themes in the book were a little too "grown-up."

One night I tried an experiment with my children. I got out my wonderful book called *Children's Book of Verse*[2] a collection of poems by various authors. (I would like to add that I would not put this book into the hands of my children as it does have many poems that are against some of our beliefs. I will, however, select poems myself to read to them.) The kids were all wound up, bouncing off the walls, and crawling all around the room. I told the children (to get their reaction) that I was going to read them some poetry. "Oh, Mom, do you have to?"

The first poem I selected was a poem about a hippopotamus. It was aptly called, "The Hippopotamus" by Jack Prelutsky. They loved it. They were fairly attentive as I read through the poem, but they were still wound up.

I read another poem, at their request. My children all love animals, so I chose another poem about animals. This one was called, "The Tiger" by William Blake. This time the poem was profound. I asked them to explain the poem to me. They said, "Read it again." I read the poem again and they still did not get it. Again they said, "Read it *one more time*." This time, they were able to answer the question the author was asking in the poem.

I closed the book and said, "Time for bed."

They responded with, "Oh, Mom, can't you read one more?" (You may be thinking that my children were just practicing the fine art of "bedtime-stalling-tactics," but at this moment I could tell that they honestly desired to hear more poetry.)

This time I chose a poem that was definitely a quiet-down poem. I told them they had to be very quiet while I read. The poem I chose was called "Bedtime" by Thomas Hood. It was a marvelous poem. I read the poem gradually, making my voice softer and softer. When I got to the last line, "It's Time for Little Children to Go to Bed," I was speaking just barely over a whisper. When I looked up from the book, all the children were content and quiet.

If anyone had walked into my home at that moment they would not have believed eight children were sitting in the living room. You could barely hear more than their breathing. In a few short minutes, reading poetry had turned my bouncy, wound-up kids into quiet and calm children who were prepared to go to bed.

The first time I told Ashley I wanted her to read a classic, she looked at me with a sideways look as if to say, "Are you crazy?" Of course, she would never really say that, but she does on occasion think it. Now when she asks me what the book is about and I respond with, "It's a classic!" she no longer looks at me sideways. But looks at me thankfully...sometimes.

NOTES

1. If you are interested in finding out more about Charlotte Mason, you can find information at:
   http://homepage.bushnell.net/~peanuts/CMason.html
2. *A Children's Book of Verse.* 1987. Newmarket, England: Brimax Books.

HOW TO MOVE WHEN IN PARK

Have you ever sat in your car, pushed on the gas pedal to go forward, but instead nothing happened? After revving your engine awhile, you looked down and realized you were sitting in Park.

Sometimes I feel like I'm going through life just revving my engine. I think I'm getting somewhere, but when I look at the road, the scenery is the same. If the scenery is really nice, I might enjoy just sitting there in Park. If the road ahead seems scary or even unpleasant, it's very difficult to raise my hand up to the gearshift and move it into Drive. Sometimes life is like that. We might see the task that looms ahead of us, and we just want to sit there in Park.

With eight children I have had some pretty rough nights. When light through yonder window breaks, I'd rather pull the shades. When a child appears at the door and whines, "I'm hungry," I'd rather toss him a bagel and say, "Fetch!" But we can't go through life in Park. We need to shift ourselves into Drive.

Often, the drive that mom has is what drives the home. We need to be ever mindful what gear we are in. It is especially important in terms of our husbands. As their helpmeets, that sometimes means we need to get in the driver's seat and put the car in gear. Let's look at the following scenario of a mom in Park.

Her husband comes home from a long day at work. He is met by a wife who nonchalantly says, "Oh hi," and children who don't seem to notice he's home. The television is blaring; supper is not even a thought in his wife's mind, and he wonders why he's there? Dad then decides he too would like to be in Park.

What can a mom do to help a dad get into Drive? Do you send your husband off to work with a hug, and a "have a good day"? Or do you not even seem to notice he has left? I've become increasingly convinced that how we treat our husbands has a direct reflection on the motivation of everyone in the home.

If Steve comes home and trips on something, his motivation for the rest of the evening is pretty much gone. If I get into Drive and clean up before he gets home, it helps him enjoy the rest of his evening.

It makes his night to be greeted by us. It is something so simple, yet it creates a mood for him. There are many times a week that the whole family gathers inside the door waiting for Daddy to walk in. Sometimes he stops outside to pet the dogs or the cats, while we wait impatiently inside. We decide before he comes in what we will say. Sometimes, if it's Friday, we all shout, "Happy Weekend!" Sometimes we shout, "We love You!" Or, "You're the best dad in the whole world!"

Believe me, these are the types of things that motivate my husband. He is motivated out of love for us. If we take the time to show him that we love him, he's more likely to fix the leaky faucet. If I'm affectionate to him, he will do just about anything. But if I'm ignoring him, not on purpose but because I'm busy, he definitely has a harder time helping out or even wanting to be awake. He'd rather take a nap, if his family won't talk to him.

One way to get yourself out of Park is to find out what motivates you. It is also helpful to know what motivates those around you. As the home manager, I need to know how to help our family get out of Park.

I am more motivated when I'm alone. This makes it very difficult for me to get things done when I have eight people around all day long. My motivation is *silence*. If I have a really big task ahead of me, I will often sit revving my engine until I can get some time to work alone. So the hallway that needs painting waits until all the kids are grown, or I guess I could ship them off to Grandma's for a few days.

If I want to shift Ashley into Drive, all I have to do is turn on some music. If we have boppy music on the stereo, she gets a lot done. However, *I* end up dancing around the living room with a child in my arms. So it doesn't necessarily work for me.

Some children are motivated by threats of punishment. Some are motivated by rewards. Some people can only get motivated after being totally embarrassed by someone. A close relative of mine did her best work when someone close to her made her cry. Isn't that sad? Basically she did the best work when she feared failure in the eyes of someone else. The people who feel compelled to clean, only for company, are motivated out of their desire to please others. It might do us some good to evaluate what motivates us and what motivates our children.

A very common cry of a home schooling mom is, "How can I motivate my child?" Children can be motivated in a variety of ways. One way to shift your children into Drive is to make their tasks more fun and different. You can even tie them to their tasks. I've actually tried that with one of my children who was having trouble getting the dishes done. I put a rope from one cabinet to another, and she couldn't move more than five inches in any direction. It worked for her. That also works for her in her schoolwork. I just don't let her leave the room she's working in. But I also can't let her work where there are distractions. Others easily distract her, but she is also a distraction to others. She needs to be able to tap her pencil, hum a few bars of "The Star Spangled Banner," bounce, or sit upside-down.

There is one constant factor that motivates all of my children. If I get excited about something, they get excited about it, too. But I can't always be excited about *everything*. What motivates us doesn't necessarily motivate our children. We need to be careful not to use only one kind of motivation with them all.

Remember the boy in class who would raise his hand almost every time the teacher would start a lesson and say, "Is this gonna be on the test?" His motivation for listening was to pass the test. I don't necessarily think passing the test should be the goal. Shouldn't a child just want to learn everything in his environment that he can possibly learn? So how do you motivate them to love to learn?

The biggest way, of course, is to model it. If you spend all of your time in front of the TV, chances are, that's what your child is going to see as being important. If you get excited about reading something new and share it with your family, they will catch the excitement.

The "Bean" game is one of my favorite inspirational tools. In this game you have a certain number of beans, each representing a certain amount of money, or a certificate of some kind. That's up to you. You keep the beans in something like an egg carton. Put all the beans on one side of the egg carton. Every time you have to tell your child to do a certain thing, you simply move a bean to the other side of the egg carton. At the end of a specified period of time, the child gets to cash in the beans.

I personally think this game should be called the "Mommy-Doesn't-Lose-It" game because it is very calming. There is no yelling. There are no threats issued. If the child doesn't do what he's supposed to do, he loses a bean.

Another motivator is a chart. Some children like to fill out their charts, or flip their cards, or add check marks. I have index boxes with chore cards for each of the children. The only problem is the index cards and boxes have never been implemented because I can't get out of Park.

Some kids simply want us to tell them they are doing a good job. Those are the easy kids. Except if we never tell them they are doing a good job, then they may quit trying.

Bryan will do anything for applause. He will probably be the type of child who just needs me to pat him on the back to keep spurring him on while he works.

Some children are motivated by peers. This is a little harder in a home school setting. You might need to explore ways to have contests with other kids who are also motivated by peers.

If you take the time to learn about your children, shifting them into Drive will be a joy rather than a drag. Your children will soon learn how to shift themselves into Drive, and then you will be able to sit back and enjoy the ride.

Chapter
12

HABITS TO BREAK!
HABITS TO MAKE!

Picture the following scene with me. The pastor is in front of the church taking prayer requests. Little Johnny in the second row is waving his hand wildly. "Yes, Johnny, do you have an item of prayer or praise this morning?"

"Yes, Pastor, I do. Could you please pray for my Mom?" Johnny says with sincerity.

"Is your mom sick, Johnny?" The preacher asks.

"Oh no, she's fine. But could you just pray that she wouldn't yell at us so much when we're getting ready to come to church?"

All eyes in the church glance over at Johnny's mom. Of course they can't see her because she has hidden herself under the pew.

As much embarrassment as that would bring, what Johnny did is sort of what should be done to help someone with a bad habit. Sometimes the only way out of a bad habit is through prayer.

Naturally I don't advocate little children airing the family's "dirty laundry" at church, but wouldn't it sometimes be nice to know a whole body of saints are praying for you to break a habit that has found a foothold in your life?

Bad habits are an area in our lives that we like to keep hidden from people. Why is that? Why don't we want anyone to know that we eat ice cream every night before we go to bed and that is why we weigh more than we want? Why would we be embarrassed for someone to hear that we don't read our Bible every day? Why are we too proud to ask for prayer about something that is vital in our walk with God? I firmly believe that if we get the backing of prayer, we can break any habit or develop good habits.

Shortly after beginning to attend a church in California, I was at a prayer meeting when I felt the Holy Spirit prompt me to ask for prayer to give up smoking. I sat in my seat silently. He continued prompting me. Still I sat. In my mind I was wrestling with many thoughts. Among those thoughts was the fear that I would be confessing a *sin* to people who were godly saints. The pastor's wife kept praying,

"Lord, there is someone here who needs prayer. Please encourage this person to ask."

Ahhh, she's talking about me! I screamed within my head.

Meekly I said, "I think it's me. I think I need prayer." I then spilled my guts and told them that I was a smoker. They prayed for me, and I felt "delivered."

The next morning I forgot I was "delivered" and went down to the store and bought another pack of cigarettes. That afternoon a dreadful thing happened. I was out in the garage smoking (I had left four children under the age of five alone in the house) when Ashley came out to tell me that Cathy had drunk some of David's medicine. I ended up having to rush her to the emergency room to drink some charcoal. That charcoal stuff is horrible.

That cigarette I had smoked in the garage earlier was the last cigarette I ever smoked. I had tried quitting before, but never had I tried with the help of the brethren and God.

Several months later I was privileged to pray for a sister in our church who was also trying to break the cigarette habit. She told me before I began to pray for her, "I was so impressed when you spoke up for God to deliver you, but I was too chicken to let them know I smoked and needed prayer, too."

If prayer helped me break my habits, why shouldn't I use prayer with my children to help them break their habits?

Often I see people who want to spank the habits out of their children. They forget a key component. They forget to ask God for help. I'll even go further to say, they forget to ask their children to help.

We have tried this habit-breaking approach a few times with our children, and I firmly believe it works. This is what we do.

When I notice one of my children has developed a "habit," the first thing I do is pray for wisdom and guidance. I then take that child aside and tell her the habit that I have seen in her. The next step I believe is very important. I then ask her if she thinks it is a habit that she would like God to help her conquer. If she says, "Yes!" we move on to prayer. We pray together. Then I ask her what I can do to help her break her habit.

Let's say she has a habit of forgetting to put the dishes in the dishwasher. I have decided that I am not going to make her eat off dirty plates. I'm obviously not going to do them myself. So what should we do? She tells me that she thinks if I come to her, no matter where she is or what she is doing, and give her a clue word, then that will help her to remember.

We try it for a few days. The first couple of days, as we are finishing dinner, I say to her, "Rumplestiltzkin!" That reminds her that she needs to put the dishes in the dishwasher after she rinses them off.

After a couple of days, I stop giving her the clue word. She does pretty well for a couple of days. Then I notice that she once again has left the dishes in the sink. I yell up the stairs to her bedroom the clue word…"Rumplestiltzkin!" Immediately she comes down the stairs and completes her job. After about a week, she no longer needs to hear the clue word.

Sometimes a child will say he would like me to touch him lightly on the shoulder and remind him he is not doing what he is supposed to be doing. This virtually eliminates the "Nagging Mom Syndrome." It also eliminates the "I'm Getting So Mad At This Child Syndrome."

The only problem I run into with this method of habit training is when the child thinks it would be beneficial to him if I dump a pot of spaghetti on his head to remind him that he hasn't taken a bath in four weeks.

You may think that this method of habit training is too time-consuming. You will have to be ever watchful that your children are doing what they are supposed to do. You cannot even let them get away with it even one time. They are just like a smoker who takes one puff, then—Bam!—he's right back into smoking again.

If you continue to hold your child accountable over a period of time, the habit he is trying to develop will become ingrained in him. He will no longer need to be reminded, but he will carry out the habit naturally without much thought.

Not only is habit-breaking important, but habit-making is also essential if you want to encourage growth and maturity in your children.

There are a lot of habits I would like to see my children develop like making their beds when first rising in the morning, saying please and thank you, drinking lots of water throughout the day. Those habits don't really have any impact on their relationship with the Lord, but they do make a difference. I also want them to develop habits that please the Lord like tithing cheerfully, attending church regularly, and praying daily.

Do we consider developing spiritual habits in our children worthy of the time it takes for our children to learn them? It doesn't come naturally for many people to spend time with the Lord everyday, but if a child is trained in this area, it will be a lifelong habit that he will not have to struggle with (like I do).

I challenge you to examine your children. Find their habits that are weak and pluck them out, one by one. Discover what lifelong habits you want your children to have and cultivate them. They won't develop a good habit by being nagged into it, but by constant encouragement.

So, the next time your child is sitting at the table, his desk, or wherever, gazing out the window, don't walk up and smack him upside the head. Gently lay your hand upon his shoulder. And when he looks up at you, give him the look that says, "You're dawdling, Dear." Don't give him a look that says, "You better get back to work or else!"

If we give our children nothing else in life but a love for the Lord Jesus Christ and strong character, we will have succeeded as parents. Character will get him a job. Character will get him up in the morning when he would rather not get up. Character will hold his marriage together someday. If we as parents build strong, godly character traits into our children, they will have the potential to bring about powerful change in our country in the future.

If you desire your children to have strong character, make it a habit to help them develop good habits and eliminate bad habits.

Chapter

13

PASSIONS

I wonder if God is grieved when we don't pursue the passions He has given us? Steve and I were watching a movie one night about an astronomer who manned a telescope out in the middle of nowhere, searching the sky night after night for the appearance of a strange phenomenon. When someone asked the astronomer why she continued working at a job that offered little pay, no respect, and no opportunity for her to fulfill her potential, she responded by saying, "It is my passion!"

Some people say that moms are not fulfilling their potential when they stay at home changing poopy diapers and wiping snotty noses all day. The world says, "Go get a job and bring home the bacon! The workplace will bring you satisfaction and fulfillment."

My response to the world is, "I may be under-paid and stinky at times, but staying at home with my children *is* my passion!" I feel like I am one of the most blessed people on the face of the earth. As a stay-at-home mom, I am able to give in to the passions that God has given me.

My number one passion *is* my children. I just adore those little bundles. For instance, I've always known that I wanted a dozen kids. I've been passionate about it! So here we are on our way to a dozen kids.

God has also given me a passion for learning. I love to learn! I even get enthused about learning useless trivia. Did you know the Jell-O capital of the world is Des Moines, Iowa? I get excited about teaching my children at home because I get to learn new things every day.

When we were reading about the original thirteen colonies, I got so excited I almost hyperventilated. I get energized when I read about men like William Bradford. He was just an ordinary kid, but God gave him a passion. William Bradford did not give up when faced with death. He easily could have, but he didn't. The passion burned in him to boldly go where no pilgrim had gone before.

When I read about men and women of faith, I discover how God has woven events throughout history to bring about His plan. When I read about people like Benjamin Franklin and George Washington, I feel myself saluting them inside. When I read about great men and women who followed their God-given passions to help shape a better world, well, that just really revs my motor. It reveals to me that God's touch upon our lives will direct our paths toward His final goal.

God has also given me a passion for writing. I probably won't change the world with my pen (or with my computer) but if I can influence even one person to have a closer walk with God then I might be able to hear one day, "Well done, thou good and faithful servant."

I am an ordinary person, just like William Bradford was, but I too have an extraordinary God who can work mightily through me when I pursue my passions.

What stirs you? What is your passion? Are you living it? Or are you settling for what feels safe and secure? What talent has God given you? Are you using it?

As a home schooling, stay-at-home mom, I have the best of all worlds. I can live my passion, but I can also help my children pursue their passions. As we spend time together day after day, my main job is to be the Master's gardening assistant. He plants the seeds of passion in their hearts, and I get to water those passions, cultivate them, and watch them grow.

How do I water those passions? I begin by bathing my children in prayer. I pray that they will hear the voice of God. I pray they will walk with Him all the days of their lives. I pray they will listen to the inner stirrings of the Lord when in His quiet voice He whispers into their hearts, and they obey.

How do I cultivate their passions? First, I listen to them.

Find creative ways to listen to your children. Have regular "dates" with them. I recently read about a man who took his teenage daughters out on dates. He'd take them to a movie, or out for a pizza, or even go to the mall. What a marvelous way to stay in touch with your children! Once you know what really revs up your kids' engines, you can then begin to cultivate their interests!

Ashley adores animals. As long as she has been alive, she has had a pet. Now, Ashley is different than most kids when it comes to animals. She doesn't just get a puppy for the sake of having a puppy because they are "soooo" cute. This child lives and breathes caring for animals.

When she was about seven, we told her we would allow her to have a horse when she turned twelve. Well, twelve came quickly, too quickly. Rather than renege on a promise, we told her she could have a horse *if* she paid for it.

So, Ashley went to work. She worked extremely hard making bread for a local farmer's market. It wasn't long before she had enough money to buy a horse. She ended up getting two horses for the price of one. After she bought a horse, we had to build a fence and put up a lean-to. I don't recommend getting a horse before you have a fence. Just trust me on this one. One of the horses she bought was not broken to ride. Another small detail I would also not recommend. The first time I saw Ashley fly over the horse's ears, I just about had a cow. Ashley never gave up on that horse, even though I wanted her to at times. After one year of faithful training, Ashley has taken that unbroken mare and has turned her into a fine jumping horse.

Ashley would really like to have horses for the rest of her life. She doesn't see herself without them. We don't know what is in store for her future, but if it has something to do with horses, then I praise God that we were willing to put our own feelings about getting a horse aside so that she could spend time with a horse.

We can cultivate, at the expense of our own desire sometimes, or we can stamp out the passion in our children's hearts. My husband and I felt strongly led to allow Ashley to have the horse. Even though neither of us knew anything about horses. We kept considering the cost and many times wanted to break our promise. But we could not. We did not want to extinguish a fire that God may have put in her heart for purposes unknown to us.

My son John loves to draw. He illustrates long stories, then comes to me, and asks me to write the words for him. One day when he brought me a story, I asked him, "Are you going to be an author some-day?"

"No," he replied, "I'm going to make science stuff for TV."

"Hmmm...a budding scientist. How exciting!"

Up until that point I hadn't really noticed that he liked science much. When we finished typing up his story, I took him into our family library and showed him a couple of science books that I had found to be great resources. I told him that anytime he wanted me to read a science book to him, he should just ask. We then sat down together and spent about an hour perusing one of the books. He would look at the pictures and ask me to read about it. It was one of those "moments" for me that helped fuel my own passion. I saw his young eyes so bright with excitement about learning new things. I was almost saddened when he said, "Okay, that's enough." But I know there will be more times that we will sit down together with the science book.

I once heard a joke about a mother who went to her pastor for prayer. "I need prayer, Pastor. My son told me the other day he wants to be a 'moanback' man."

"A 'moanback' man? What's a 'moanback' man?" asked the pastor.

"It's the man who stands in the alley behind the garbage truck, waves his arm, and yells, 'Ca'moan back.'"

What would you do if your son wanted to be a "moanback" man? This is what I would do. First, I'd take him on a tour of a dump. Then, if he still wanted to do it, I'd take him "dumpster diving," let him carry the garbage out everyday for awhile, and teach him everything he ever did and did not want to know about recycling and composting. Then, if he still wanted to do it, I'd pray.

We need to let our children see the positives and the negatives of the professions they are interested in. If at all possible, we should let them spend time with someone in that profession.

Another way to cultivate your children's passions is to broaden their horizons. My daughter may love to dance around the house, but until she goes to a ballet, she may never realize how her passion could be enhanced. My son may love to draw, but until he sees some Rembrandts or VanGoghs that artistic spark within him may never become a passionate fire.

My son David and I discovered a web site that will translate languages. David wrote a letter to his grandparents, then translated it into Spanish. He then e-mailed it to them. They, in turn, e-mailed another letter back to him in Spanish. He found this fascinating! After he wrote a second letter back to them, he said, "I think I would like to study languages."

I don't want my children selecting their professions based on worldly opinions. I want them choosing their professions based on the passions that God has given them. I want them to know God has called them to that profession for a purpose.

I may have a child grow up to be a linguist who translates the Bible, taking the Scriptures to little-known villages. I may have a son who becomes a scientist who sends shock waves through the scientific community because he has proven evolution to be convoluted. Or perhaps, just maybe, I might have a child who grows up to be a "moanback" man, praying for the people whose garbage he collects.

WE INTERRUPT THIS LIFE...

One spring morning, I woke up full in inspiration: I decided I was going to get organized! I thought to myself, *No more undone tasks for me, no sir! No more chore charts without checkmarks next to them! No more dust on the windowsills! My life is going to run smoothly without incident or interruption!*

I began my new journey toward organization by writing a "to do" list. The difference with this "to do" list and countless other lists I had written before was that I was determined not to lose this list. I began jotting down the things I wanted to get done over the next couple of days. There were mountains of laundry that were beginning to ferment, all the rooms in the house that desperately needed to be spring-cleaned, a tilled garden plot that was ready to be planted, a half-built chicken coop that clucked to be completed so we could get some long awaited chickens, and a chapter that needed to be written. The list didn't even include the children getting their schoolwork done.

I decided to start with the most urgent task—laundry. When the laundry was getting somewhat under control, I decided to clean the easiest rooms first. Briana and Erica didn't have very much: two beds, two dressers, a couple boxes of toys and a box of stuffed animals. However, it was quite astonishing to me how messy two little girls with hardly any junk could be.

I put all their clothes away, refolded the clothes that had mysteriously become unfolded in their drawers, and looked in the closet. It was still in order. I finished their room, went on to John and David's room. I threw away the garbage they had been saving—toilet paper tubes, Kleenex boxes, even a Pop-Tart box. *How'd they get that?* I wondered.

Then I went to tackle the office. I thought this would be the next easy place. The problems began when I realized I only had room in my file cabinet for about three more pieces of paper, but I had four inches of papers to file.

My first thought was *Quick! Call Steve and have him bring home a new file cabinet.* But then I remembered my goal—*Don't store, get rid of more!* So I plunged into the dreaded, over-stuffed file cabinet and ruthlessly purged the files. *Wow, I really have some good stuff in here*, I thought as I tossed most of it into the trash. I vowed not to bring any more pieces of paper into the house.

After I finished the file cabinet, I began on the bookshelf. Ashley walked by and heard me muttering out loud to myself, "I don't need this book...I don't need this book...I'll *never* read this book...Why do I have this book on the shelf?" Books are one of Ashley's favorite things. She has learned that books are to be cherished. She apparently didn't think I was practicing what I preached since I was tossing all of those great books into the Goodwill box.

She came running. "You're not going to get rid of those *books* are you? You can't get rid of books. I'll take all the books you want to get off the shelves, and I'll put them in my room."

She wasn't helping! I explained to her why I was getting rid of the books we didn't need. She left with an armload of books for her room.

I continued with the task at hand.

Do I really need these textbooks from the public schools? No! Am I going to be able to read this book before I'm sixty? No!

Out they went. I was beginning to feel a real sense of accomplishment. *Maybe I will get everything done on my list!* I thought.

Outside I went to plant the garden. I planted some broccoli, cabbage, and tomatoes. I was really feeling great as I checked off "plant the garden" on my "to do" list. The garden had been tilled and ready to plant for two weeks, but I just hadn't found the time to get out and do it.

The next morning I was determined to have things go according to plan. I had just sat down in the tub to take my bath for the morning when I heard a knock at the door.

"Who is it?"

In a frantic tone of voice Ashley yelled, "Li'l Bit is having kittens and one is hanging out!"

"What do you want me to do?" I asked.

"I want you to help her." She said on the verge of tears.

How could I put my plan for a bath ahead of our cat having kittens? I pulled the plug and got out of the tub.

Having kittens in our house causes quite an upheaval. Every time we have new kittens, I might as well just write off my plans for school. The older children are too preoccupied with checking on the new mother and counting kittens. I suppose I could still consider it "school" if they are counting, couldn't I?

The phone must have rung fifteen times that morning. Each time it seemed the caller had something urgent for me to do.

I tried to get outside to work on the chicken coop, but each time I would get ready to head out the door, the baby would start wailing to be fed.

When I finally got out the door, I tromped over to the garden to see how my plants were doing. I couldn't believe what I saw. All the plants were shriveled and frozen. A killer frost had zapped them the night before. *Uugh*, I grumbled. *If I had just checked out the forecast before I planted. But I was determined to check off one more thing on my list!*

I went back to my list. "Plant garden—again!" I added. Since I was in no mood to dig up dead plants, I decided to do another item on the list. "Work on a chapter." I sat down at my computer and could think of nothing but all the interruptions I had experienced in the last few hours. As I was just beginning to regain an attitude of thankfulness that I had children to interrupt me, I was paid a visit by our dear Briana.

Briana came in with her sock in her hand. "My sock is wet, Mom. Want to feel it?" as she thrust the wet sock into my hand.

"How did *that* happen?" I asked.

So sweetly she said, "My underwear did it."

"Yuck!"

I returned her sock with instructions for her to put it in the laundry room and to please wash her hands. I got up and did the same.

When I returned to my computer screen, I just kept staring at it. Suddenly I knew why I had all those interruptions. I had not committed my day to the Lord. I wanted to do the day *my* way. I had made *my* list without even asking the Lord if He might have some other plans for me.

All those interruptions just might have been the Lord trying to get my attention. I sometimes think that I can do all things in my own strength. I forget that my plans may not be His plans for my day, or even for my life for that matter. A Scripture from Philippians 2:12-18 came to mind:

Therefore, my beloved, as you have always obeyed, not as in my presence only, but now much more in my absence, work out your own salvation with "fear" and trembling; for it is God who works in you both to will and to do for His good pleasure.

Do all things without complaining and disputing, that you may become blameless and harmless, children of God without fault in the midst of a crooked and perverse generation, among whom you shine as lights in the world, holding fast the word of life, so that I may rejoice in the day of Christ that I have not run in vain or labored in vain.

Yes, and if I am being poured out as a drink offering on the sacrifice and service of your faith, I am glad and rejoice with you all. For the same reason you also be glad and rejoice with me.

As I contemplated these verses I realized that in all of my interruptions, I had failed to allow God to work in me. When Ashley knocked on the door as I lay there in my warm tub, I must confess, I grumbled and complained.

When the baby repeatedly needed to be fed, I was not glad and rejoicing.

After the tenth phone call about the same project, I was feeling like I was laboring in vain.

As I sat at my computer, I began to pray for God to call the shots. I asked Him if He would please e-mail me my "to do" list for the following day.

As I logged on the next morning, I half expected my e-mail from God to show up. Even though God did not send me an e-mail message, He did nudge my heart to give my day to Him. And I did.

Chapter 15

TEA TIME!

A few months ago I noticed behavioral changes in one of my girls. She wanted to spend a lot of time in her room, *alone*. Some of her attitudes were also shifting. She had normally been so helpful with the little ones, and now she didn't really want anything to do with them. I even noticed her responding with an arrogant tone of voice at times.

I decided to call up some friends who also had daughters about the same age as mine. They too had noticed changes in their daughters' behavior. As we compared notes, our suspicions were confirmed. We decided on the most likely cause—hormones! (And if you don't believe hormones affect you, just ask one of my kids at a certain time each pregnancy if I don't just "lose it" for no apparent reason.)

On a date with my husband one afternoon, I mentioned the changes that were happening in our "little" girl. He innocently asked, "How long do you think this will last?"

"Until menopause." I answered. "She probably has another forty years to go."

"Is there anything we can *do* about it?" He inquired.

"Well, I was just reading that raspberry leaf tea helps to even out hormones. It's mostly used by pregnant women, but it is helpful in young women, too."

"Can you buy it in bulk?" he asked. "Maybe all of you could drink it?"

Very funny. Actually, I'm not a big fan of tea. The thought of drinking it didn't really appeal to me. I would have to somehow make it fun. But how could I make drinking tea fun?

Then it dawned on me—*We need "tea time."* I started picturing in my mind my two oldest daughters and I having a nice peaceful time every day, drinking our tea together after I put all the little ones down for a quiet time. It would be "our" time together.

I decided each daughter would join the tea party at age ten. (Even though I secretly hoped their hormones would not start raging until they were at least eleven.)

My good intentions to have tea time alone with my daughters were thwarted the first day. Apparently one of the little children had gotten wind of the plans for a tea party. Of course, they were sure they would be invited for tea. Our tea for three ended up being tea for the whole tribe. It wasn't quite what I had in mind, but the tea party turned out to be one of those special moments for all of us. Briana showed us how mannerly she could be when she said in her sweetest voice ever, "This tea is delightful. May I please have some more?"

Even the boys got in on the act. (They never want to be left out of anything.) There they sat, six little children around the table drinking tea with their pinkies extended.

Memories are different than traditions. Although both can be intertwined, traditions are carried on, but memories are carried within. Someday when my children are watching their own children have tea time, I wonder if they will get a far off look in their eyes as they drift back to memories of pinkies and raspberry leaf tea? Will smiles creep across their faces, as if they have a special secret? That is really what memories are…special secrets.

Will they remember the Christmas Mom spent hundreds of dollars on gifts? Or will they only remember the day after Christmas when she made snow angels with them?

Will they remember a kitchen full of dirty dishes? Or will they think of all those meals with homemade whole wheat bread every time they smell fresh bread?

Will they remember that they had ground beef every Tuesday? Or will they remember the day every meal was blue? I still remember when my mom made green mashed potatoes, and I must have only been two or three.

For John's birthday this year he asked for green eggs and ham for his birthday meal. He obviously had remembered the time we had green eggs and ham while I read Dr. Seuss's book *Green Eggs and Ham*. He wanted to once again experience the enjoyment of that dinner together.

It doesn't take a lot of time, energy, or imagination to help create memories. We can make memories during school time as well. School doesn't have to be dull. Make learning fun. Children love to play games. Games provide a creative way to teach kids facts that might otherwise be laborious to memorize.

When my kids were studying the human body, we made body part cards. It was similar to the game of "Head Bone." On each card we wrote the name of a body part. Once the cards were completed, it was time to "play." We had two kids stand side by side. One was allowed to draw a card. "Clavicle!" he shouted. Then the other child picked a card. "Tibia!" he yelled. We laughed as they tried to figure out if one should bend his clavicle to the other's tibia, or if one should lift the tibia to the clavicle. The next card chosen was "patella" followed by "sternum." When they tried to *connect* the patella to the tibia, they fell in a heap. We laughed so hard, we cried. They couldn't wait to play the game again. They still talk about that game!

Think back to when you were in school. What memories stand out to you? You probably recall something you did that was out of the ordinary. I remember going outside and role playing that I was Socrates and the rest of the class were my pupils. If I had only read about Socrates in a book, I probably would not be able to pinpoint a time when I learned about him. That experience taught me that most learning happens through self-discovery. Learning is not just being told the "facts."

The opportunities to make lasting impressions are endless. Our kids don't have to read books sitting in a chair at their desks. Sometimes my kids and I hop on my bed with a book and read. Sometimes we read in the living room or at the kitchen table having a snack. We have considered reading in the bathtub (in our swimsuits), but decided all eight of us might be a tight squeeze. Sometimes we read outside in the backyard or lying on a blanket at the park. As a little insect crawls across the pages of a book, a child discovers for himself how many legs an insect has. And sometimes how loud a mom can scream.

Have you ever watched eight children read about Abe Lincoln while wearing a fake beard? Have you ever gone outside and measured how big

Noah's ark really was? Have you ever reenacted a story from the Bible?

Have you ever watched your children pretend they were peasants living during the reign of Queen Mary? If not, you have probably never had the chance to witness a peasant revolt in your own home. When the Queen sent out a decree that all Protestants must recant or lose their heads, my little peasants went wild. I must say the Protestant Reformation is no longer just a hazy seven-syllable concept in their minds. Their understanding of that period in time was enlightened when they had to walk in the shoes of peasants past and discover what it would be like to have to die for their beliefs.

Unlike Detective Joe Friday in Dragnet, our motto is not "Just the facts, please." Don't get me wrong, we must teach our children facts, but we don't have to teach them in a "closed" classroom environment. With a little imagination, we can make learning memorable.

Let's say you have a child working on multiplication. At lunch you write out a simple menu for her. She has to check her menu, then set the table for each person using the right amount from her menu. The menu might look like this: 3 x 0 knives, 3 x 1 forks, 3 x 2 apple sections, and (3 x 2)-5 glasses of milk.

Get the idea? Intertwine learning with the mundane and create a memory. The possibilities are endless.

Wake the kids up one morning by yelling at the top of your lungs, "Wake up! It's Purple Day!" For the rest of the day everyone has to wear purple, eat purple, drink purple, spell purple, write purple, read purple. You could even do a purple experiment. Live purple for the day.

Go for the memory!

Ask God to help you create memorable moments. You will be surprised at what He comes up with.

Last Mother's Day I decided I was not going to be let down. (That can happen you know.) I was asking the Lord to help me not to be disappointed when a thought came to me. I was going to make Mother's Day a great day for my children. I awoke feeling like it was going to be the best Mother's Day possible. Do you know what I did? I decided to use it as an opportunity to really spoil my children. Hey, I'm allowed. It's Mother's Day!

So much of what we do as mothers is service and correcting. I decided it would be fun to spoil. When asked where I wanted to eat, I said, "McDonalds! The one with a play place!" The whole day I spoiled those children. We went shopping at the mall, and I allowed them to have a chocolate from the chocolate store. I even let them ride on the fifty-cent rides. After dinner we went to Dairy Queen, and they got ice cream.

We pretty much limit everything in our house. When we give M & M's, they get five, not a handful, not a whole package. They get five. If they are allowed to have pop, they must share the can three ways. If they get any kind of special snack, it's usually a small amount.

I didn't know how much this day had meant to my kids. I had even forgotten I had done it until the other day when one of my children reminded me about the day they "got spoiled." I didn't have a clue what Cathy was talking about, so she had to remind me of all the details. She told me, "Don't you remember? You took us to McDonalds, and even to the mall. We walked around the mall for a long time. Then you even let us each pick out a chocolate from that store with chocolates. You never even let us go in that store before. But that day you let us each pick something. I got a caramel on a stick. It was so good. Then you let us all ride on those rides in the middle of the mall. We had so much fun! And after, we went to Dairy Queen and got our *own* ice cream. Don't you remember Mom?"

I had tears in my eyes as I heard her recall the day I spoiled them. She didn't sound spoiled, she sounded grateful.

She then said, "Do you think we could do that again sometime?"

"Of course not," I said, as I rumpled her hair. "You can only get spoiled once in your lifetime. You might have already gotten too spoiled. Let me check." Then I looked behind her ears as if looking for something. "Well," I said, "You don't have any green fuzzy stuff growing behind your ears. I guess you're not too spoiled yet. Maybe we can do it again sometime."

She then squeezed me tight. She ran off to play but quickly hurried back. She grabbed my head and looked behind my ears. "I guess you're not too spoiled yet either, Mommy."

Part

GOD
MOMENTS

Three

16

ON MY KNEES!

Have you ever secretly identified with the women who just "up and leave" their families, who are gone without a trace? When people say, "How could a mom ever do such a thing?" have you ever thought to yourself, *I wonder if that will be my story on the news someday?*

As much as I hate to admit it, I have imagined myself walking down the airport terminal destined for a place of peace, tranquility, and simplicity.

I seem to want to escape to a deserted island, particularly when I have a nearly two-year-old in the house. I have been training the babe since birth to obey my every command, and then suddenly the child looks me in the eye and says, "No!" That's my ticket. I do not like hearing the word "no" from my child. It means only one thing. It means there is going to be a test, and I better come out with an A+ or I might as well board the plane.

Ashley was very compliant as a toddler. Then Christi came along and corrupted her. I think Christi would whisper into Ashley's ear what the next "plan" was. Christi and Ashley often put me to the test, and many times I failed.

When Christi and Ashley were two and three-years old, we had just moved to a new town. Ten days before we moved, I had Cathy by C-section. The doctor instructed me I was not to go up or down any stairs for six weeks. For some reason we rented an apartment with stairs. It was a tiny apartment. You know the kind—you can sit on the couch on one side of the room and change channels on the television without a remote from the other side of the room.

While we lived in the apartment, Ashley and Christi pretty much had the run of the house—literally. Whenever they wanted to disobey me, they would just bolt up the stairs because they knew I could not run after them. Needless to say, I lost their respect very quickly.

Finally we purchased a house and mom could now *run*! I decided it was time to once again lay down the law. In the apartment, the kids just played all day instead of taking naps because I didn't have the energy to make them go to bed.

My first tactic to regain my post as commander in charge was to reinstitute naptime. The first day of the new naptime is one Mommy Memory that I will never forget. It was definitely a "buy me a one-way ticket" day. I tucked the girls into their beds and quietly closed the door. A few minutes later as I walked by their room, I could hear a squeaking noise. I opened the door and there were two very happy children jumping on their beds, trying to touch the ceiling. I scolded them and told them to get back in their beds. They got back under the covers, so I closed the door. This time I stood outside the door and listened. A few seconds later I heard giggling and *squeak, squeak, squeak.*

I threw open the door and screamed. "Girls, get back in bed or else I'm going to…" "Kill" was the only word I could think of at the moment. Instead of taking me seriously, they just laughed at me and continued to jump. I was quickly overtaken with a desire to hurt them. I left them jumping as I ran out of the room crying.

I knew at that moment I needed a one-way ticket. I had had it with being a mommy. Not only was I sleep-deprived from taking care of a newborn, I couldn't even make two little girls take a nap. I felt my life was spinning wildly out of my control. I was so desperate; I called a crisis hotline. Can you believe the person who answered the hotline told me there was *no one* available to talk to me? She told me to phone 9-1-1. So I did.

Now I must tell you I did not know anything about child training at the time. The only way I knew how to make my children obey was through anger. When I phoned 9-1-1, the dispatcher asked me if I had a gun. I was stunned by the question. "I don't want to *kill* them. I just want them to take a nap." I said.

"We'll send someone right over," she said. Two policemen came and checked out everything. Basically they told me they didn't think I was at risk of actually harming my children. I was just under a lot of stress.

They called a pastor and asked him to visit with me. I didn't want to visit with a pastor. I just wanted a one-way ticket to the Bahamas. Well, the pastoral visit was actually good for me, and I cancelled my plans for a lifetime getaway.

Sometimes the most trivial tasks (such as washing the dishes) can turn into "one-way ticket" days. One morning I had forgotten to buy soap for the dishwasher, so I told Ashley to use some Tide instead. Soon after she turned it on, the dishwasher began to sound "funny."

I pondered what I should do but then thought, *It's not like you turn off an appliance every time it makes a funny sound. And if I turn it off, I will have to do all the dishes by hand!*

I continued to let it run. Boy, did it run—all over the floor. Suds and water were pouring out all over the carpet that I had spent "hours" cleaning a few days earlier.

I ran into the laundry room for some dirty towels and squished them up under the dishwasher, continuing to let it run. I just kept telling myself, *I am not going to wash all those dishes by hand!*

As I was kneeling on the floor, trying to "will" the water to stop pouring all over the floor, I began pitying myself. *I hate this job! I'm sick of wet, smelly carpet. I hate having carpet in the kitchen.* I began feeling all alone in a house of ten. I began thinking of all the "things" that I do like washing dishes, dirty clothes, fixing breakfast, lunch, *and* dinner, every single day. I wash hair and little pink bottoms. I wash windows, mirrors, and toilets. I am constantly cleaning messes that I never make.

I was having a major case of PPMS (Poor Pitiful Me Syndrome). Then I began to think of all the things that I really wanted to do, but never got a chance to do, like sitting all afternoon reading a book on the couch, driving anyplace I would like to go without having to make babysitting arrangements. I even considered where I would go with my "one-way ticket."

Being the household janitor wasn't my vision of being a wife and a mom. My vision seemed a little happier, a little less messy, with a lot fewer things going wrong to mess up everything.

Then a realization hit me like a ton of bricks: Being *a servant to my family is where the Lord wants me. He wants me to spend my time serving my family. He wants me to die to myself and serve them, thereby serving Him!*

Before the dishwasher episode, the Lord had been trying to get my attention. Several times while I was driving alone in my van, all of a sudden I would be overwhelmed with a feeling that I needed to pull over, get out of my car, and get on my face before God.

Now, do you think I obeyed the Lord? No, I didn't. The sheer craziness of the idea held me back; however, I could have gone straight home, found a place to be alone with God and gotten on my face then and there. But as soon as I walked in the door there would be groceries to put away, kids who needed to be fed, and housework that needed to be done. Falling on my face before the Lord would somehow just escape my mind.   Because I failed to listen in the quiet moments, the Lord had to use an overflowing dishwasher to get my attention. There I was on my hands and knees crying my heart out to God as water poured out of the dishwasher, and a two-year-old climbed on my back yelling, "Moooommmmmyyyyy!" I began to cry.

"What do you want me to do, Lord?" I moaned.

His reply was so loud it sounded as if He was right next to me. He said, "I want you on your knees! I don't care if you're wearing a skirt or jeans. I want you on your knees! It doesn't matter if you're tired or overwhelmed. I want you on your knees! Broken dishwasher, plumbing problems, "tantrumming" toddlers, soaked kitchen carpet doesn't matter. I want you on your *knees*!"

It was at that moment I got on my face before Him. I begged Him to change my attitude. I asked Him to show me how to serve my family in a more godly way. I pleaded with Him to come in and wash all the filth out of me. As I lay there weeping, He spoke His Word to me.

"Come now, and let us reason together," says the LORD. "Though your sins are like scarlet, they shall be as white as snow; though they are red like crimson, they shall be as wool. If you are willing and obedient, you shall eat the good of the land…" (Isaiah 1:18-19)

I thanked the Lord for hearing my prayers and secretly hoped He would see fit to bless me with a *round-trip* ticket to the Bahamas.

Chapter

17

WAIT

But those who wait on the Lord shall renew their strength; they shall mount up with wings like eagles; they shall run and not be weary; they shall walk, and not faint. (Isaiah 40:31)

Have you ever heard about the man who went to the confessional and told the priest, "I need more patience—will you please pray for me?"

The priest said, "I will gladly pray for you." He began his prayer, "Father, give him tribulations in the morning, tribulations in the noontime, and tribulations in the evening…"

When you ask the Lord to make you a patient person, get ready *to wait*. Patient people have learned "the art of waiting."

I used to joke that I prayed for patience and received Ashley, Christi, Cathy, David, John, Briana, and Erica. When I found out I was pregnant with Bryan, I said, "Lord, am I not patient enough yet?" I was not serious, of course.

Because I have a lot of children, people automatically assume I have a lot of patience. Ha! The Lord just thought I needed more work in this area, that's all. I have by no means "arrived." The fourth time a child wakes me up from my nap to ask if he can have a cookie will oftentimes send me into orbit. The tenth time the three-year-old colors on the table will frequently turn me into a crazy woman who behaves as if she has never heard of the fruits of the Spirit.

To teach my children patience, I have issued the decree: When mom is napping or on the phone, the answer is always *no*! Patiently waiting for Mom to get off the phone is a very hard concept to learn when you are very little and you just see Mom standing around with a toy next to her ear.

Like my children, I tend to be an "I want it *now*!" kind of person. Waiting nine months to have a baby seems like such a long time to wait. After about six months, I can't wait to have the baby. Waiting for my children to develop into "perfect" godly children is another area where my patience wavers. I want my children to learn from their mistakes the first time they make them. I don't want to have to discipline the same child over and over again for the same misbehavior. I want my kids to learn the error of their ways the first time.

I also want my children to learn concepts automatically after hearing them for the first time. Sometimes after a great home school day I will think, "Boy, the kids sure learned a lot today!" Then Steve will begin the nightly dinner routine of asking them what they learned in school today. While the kids and I were studying a unit on government, Steve asked the kids one night at dinner, "What are the three branches of government?"

No one answered, but one by one the children's eyes drifted toward the ceiling as if they were looking for an answer to fall from heaven. Then one brave soul broke the silence. "Uh…is it the presidential?" Meanwhile I'm thinking, "I can't believe they don't know this. What have I done wrong?"

I desire for my kids to "get it" the first time; and when they don't, I have to patiently go back over the same concept and review it over and over again. This is one method God uses to teach me patience on a daily basis. I don't know why we adults expect kids to "get it" the first time. Most adults don't have that ability. In fact, I think the older you get, the slower you get at "getting it."

As parents we often get a glimpse of how our impatient natures must appear to God.

When Erica was a twenty-month-old she loved homemade bread. She would see the bread rising on the counter and yell, "Bwed!" Try calmly telling a toddler that she must wait for the bread to rise, then she must wait for it to bake, cool, and be cut, before she can eat it. The waiting seemed unbearable to her. She would cry, "Bwed! Bwed! Bwed!" She would eventually settle for a cracker.

Because I knew exactly when the bread would be done and ready to eat, I knew that Erica's impatience was in vain. No matter how flustered and upset she became, the outcome would still be the same.

God sees our troubles in the same way. He knows the outcome. He knows when the "bwed" will be done. He knows that waiting is tough for His children. That's why He gave us this promise:

But those who wait on the Lord shall renew their strength; they shall mount up with wings like eagles; they shall run and not be weary; they shall walk, and not faint. (Isaiah 40:31)

When we "wait" in His strength, we release our emotional pain to Him. Sometimes, however, we act just like Erica. We cry out to the Lord to give us what we want when we want it. We can't figure out why He won't give us what we want. We accuse Him of ignoring us and even worse—we wonder if He really loves us. Sometimes we get so impatient we throw up our hands and say, "Forget it. I didn't really want bread. I'll just go eat crackers somewhere else." When we lose our patience and walk away from God's plan, we miss out on God's best for us. We forget that He holds our future in His hands and that if we can just wait until the "bwed" is done, we will be delighted at how His plan works out for us.

Waiting for an answer to prayer, waiting for a child to put off his foolish ways, waiting in the final weeks for a baby to be born shows us how patient we really are.

Isn't patience really just being able to put your complete faith and trust in God? Isn't patience just knowing without a doubt that God will accomplish His perfect will in your life in *His* time? Isn't patience a simple act of surrender? As I surrender all that I am, into the hands of our Heavenly Father, I can be patient.

When I remember that God has a purpose for each of my children, I can be patient with them when they mess up. As long as I am listening to Him and being consistent with the children, He will complete His perfect work in them. They may not "get it" the first time, but God is not going to give up on them so neither will I.

Not long ago Bryan chose to be defiant. He was playing around, being exceptionally funny. But when I called him to come to me, he would not come. Not funny. He just stood where he was and looked at me. Ashley looked at me and said, "Oh Mom! He's being so cute, can't you ignore it?"

"Of course I can't ignore it. If I did, I would be a negligent parent." I replied with great wisdom. It would have definitely been easier at that moment to ignore his disobedience, but I knew that as a parent you either suffer now or suffer much more later.

Even though I administered appropriate discipline for his actions, he remained steadfast. After the fifteenth time I called Bryan to come, he picked up a toy and threw it at me. I was grieved! Never, had that happened in all of my parenting. When Bryan threw the toy at me, Steve stepped in and told Bryan that he must apologize to me. Again Bryan was steadfast. He refused to obey his daddy's request. It was time for the children to go to bed, so Steve put the rest of the children to bed while I continued with Bryan's training.

I could feel myself getting angry at his defiance. I prayed for the Lord to give me patience. Immediately the Lord answered my prayer. I felt a supernatural peace come over me. I no longer felt like throwing a toy back at Bryan, but I was disappointed that he would not obey me. When Steve came down the stairs after putting the children to bed, I had tears in my eyes. I told him I could not go on. I told him that I just could not continue disciplining Bryan. I was ready to give up.

Then Steve said, "Let's pray for him." I picked Bryan up in my arms. He stiffened as I picked him up. He did not want anything to do with me. We sat on the couch and Steve placed his hand on Bryan's head and began to pray. Almost immediately Bryan became relaxed. Steve's prayer brought more tears to my eyes. Throughout the ten-minute prayer, Bryan was relaxed. I almost thought he had fallen asleep while Steve prayed. When Steve concluded his prayer with "Amen," Bryan immediately said, "Amen." He then quickly said, "Sorry Mommy, Daddy."

I began to weep as I saw the power of God act in our son's life. Even though Bryan was only twenty-three-months old, God cared enough to bring him and his mom to a place of surrender.

Chapter

18

LABOR OF LOVE

Briana Sue Camp: September 3, 1994
7 pounds, 13 ounces, 19 inches long

Briana's story begins twelve months after the birth of her brother John. John was our fifth child—our third born by Cesarean section. A week after he was born, my husband and I decided we would not have any more children. This was not something we decided lightly.

I grieved that I would never give birth again. The births were just getting too hard on me. I did not think my body could go through another Cesarean. I knew in my heart that I wanted God to choose our family size, but at what cost? Even my desire for a dozen children was not quite enough to keep this up. Although we made that decision, we didn't do anything to prevent a pregnancy. It was just a decision made without any action.

In November we went to a healing crusade. Steve wrote on a prayer request card, "Please pray that Terri will be able to have our next baby naturally without having to have a C-section."

What happened to me that night in the awesome presence of God?

I was not pregnant at that time, but within the next couple of weeks I did get pregnant. We decided, after consulting with our doctor, that we would pray for a natural delivery, but would schedule a Cesarean. (I really like my life planned.)

In my sixth month of pregnancy, Steve and I decided that if we were going to pray for a miracle, we should at least believe that God answers prayer. The next day a friend told me she had been impressed in her prayer time to pray for a natural delivery for me. This confirmed to me that I was to act on God's promise. I talked at length with my doctor. We decided together that we would not schedule a C-section after all. I would be treated as if it were my first pregnancy. We strongly felt that scheduling the C-section was not fully relying on God.

The next months were an agonizing wait. What was going to happen? Would I go into labor? How should I plan for help around the house? My mom had said she would come. Then she couldn't. My sister said she would come, but she couldn't. Perhaps I wouldn't need their help?

The last month was awful. I felt miserable and extremely tired, but mostly I just didn't know what was going to happen. I had many contractions at regular intervals, but they would always stop.

The last week I had contractions a greater portion of each day and night. On Friday, I had my regular checkup. It was the first time I had to take the elevator instead of the stairs. My doctor asked me if I would like to be induced.

I said, "Yes!"

Induction began at 3:30 P.M. on Friday. Contractions came at regular intervals, but they were only moderate. We decided to keep going through the night. I couldn't get much sleep, but I wasn't in much pain.

At 6:00 A.M. on Saturday, my water broke. When I was checked, they said I hadn't dilated and the baby's head was still not engaged. An hour later the contractions became noticeably stronger.

At 8:30 A.M., I asked Steve to get me something for the pain in my hands. Yes, I was having contractions, but the pain in my hands was unbearable. I could stay on top of a contraction, but I could not deal with muscle spasms in my hands. Knowing the baby's head hadn't dropped, I figured I was now just biding my time until they wheeled me in and took the baby out through Cesarean. The doctor came by, and I told him I wanted something for the pain.

The doctor checked me and said I had dilated to three or four centimeters. We were ecstatic. When we asked about the baby's head, he said it was down where it was supposed to be. He agreed to give me a shot of something in my I.V.

I don't know what he gave me, but it was the best stuff for me. I was able to rest between what became strong contractions, but I could concentrate enough to breathe through the contractions. Steve sang praise songs to me and helped me remember that God was in charge.

An hour later, I felt the urge. I think I told Steve something like, "I think I need to push, but I'll wait until the next contraction to make sure."

"*Yes*, I think I need to push!"

The nurse came in, and sure enough, I was fully dilated and ready to birth our baby. She said she would go get the doctor. I figured I would have to pant until he came from his office.

I was sure surprised when he walked right in and said, "Okay. Go ahead and push."

"What? I'm going to have a baby?" I guess I forgot what I was there for—just for a moment, anyway.

I didn't know at the time, but my best friend, Karen, had come to the hospital to see me. She arrived just in time for Briana to be born. She quickly exited the room when she heard the doctor say, "Okay, push," and stood outside my door praying for strength for me. Her prayer was just what I needed. After twenty-eight hours without much sleep, I felt a renewed sense of strength. Minutes later, our little girl was born.

She didn't look very good when she came out. The umbilical cord was wrapped around her neck. The doctor removed it and waited for the baby to cry but she was silent. Dr. Howen turned her on her tummy in his hand and rubbed her back. (If you've ever seen the movie *101 Dalmatians*, it looked like what Roger did to revive the puppy that he thought was dead.)

The nurse reassured me she was all right, but I didn't see any sign of life. I began to feel a little panicky. Suddenly, she cried a very strong cry.

After Briana was born, I wanted to sleep for days, but the nurses kept wanting me to try to use the restroom. I did not want to use the restroom, I wanted to sleep. Then they gave me Pepsi and lots of it, but I just wanted to sleep.

They did some tests and realized that I was severely anemic. I was given two choices: I could have a transfusion, or go home and go to bed for two weeks. Of course, I opted for going to bed.

Steve's mom was able to stay with the other children and within a week I was much stronger. All my concerns before the baby was born were in vain.

God took care of my every need. He even answered Steve's prayer for our baby to be born naturally.

What happened to me that night at the Crusade in the awesome presence of God? I believe that as I stood in that auditorium, God touched me. He reached into the depths of my being and healed me from whatever had prevented me from having our last three children naturally. But even more than the physical healing, God began a work in me that was far greater than the physical. He began to work in my heart to place all my trust in Him. He showed me that He is more powerful than anything. He showed me that He cares about each one of us. It was a journey that ended with Steve and me both coming to a deeper understanding of what it means to surrender *all* areas of our lives, even our reproduction, over to Him.

19

HUNGRY?

Are you hungry for the Word of God? Do you want to feast with the Father? Do you value your Bible more than your daily bread? If your answer is no, maybe, or indifferent, perhaps you should ask yourself if you have lost your first love.

The Lord says in Revelation 2:4-5,

Nevertheless I have this against you, that you have left your first love. Remember therefore from where you have fallen; repent and do the first works, or else I will come to you quickly and remove your lampstand from its place—unless you repent.

If reading that verse doesn't send you to your knees, you better check your spiritual pulse. As I meditated on this verse, I thought back to my early days as a Christian. Christi, my second child who was an infant at the time, did not enjoy being outside the womb. She preferred being nestled in her mother's tummy where it was dark and warm. One especially difficult day (And to think I only had two children!) Christi cried and cried and cried some more.

At the time I didn't know what was wrong with her. (We found out later that she was not getting enough to eat.) After spending hours trying to soothe and comfort this little child, I finally laid her crying body in her crib and went into the bathroom. I slumped down on the floor and began to weep.

As I was crying, I heard a voice say, "Second Timothy 3:16."

I thought the voice had made a mistake, so I said, "No, it's John 3:16. I already know that verse. I learned that one in Sunday School." I must have really been stressed because I sat there, in the bathroom, having an argument with *God*!

Again the voice said, "Second Timothy 3:16."

I replied with, "There probably isn't even such a thing as Second Timothy 3:16." As soon as I said, "There probably isn't even such a thing as Second

Timothy 3:16," I knew I might be in really big trouble. Perhaps lightning would come down and strike me dead? Or maybe Steve would come in with some guys in white coats and drag me off to the place where they put people who claim to talk to God? Or maybe, just maybe, I was really talking to God, and He had something He wanted to tell me. And He wasn't going to give up until I listened to Him.

I'll never forget the kindness in the voice that echoed in my head when He said, "Second Timothy 3:16. Look it up."

I decided I didn't have anything to lose. I didn't even believe there was such a thing as Second Timothy 3:16. At that point in my life, I owned one Bible. It was a great big family Bible that was given to me as a wedding present. I plunked it on the table and looked in the Table of Contents.

"Hey, there is a Second Timothy? I wonder if there really could be a chapter three and a verse sixteen." My eyes popped open so wide when I realized such a verse existed in the Bible. I read the verse feeling like God had sent me a memo from heaven, "All Scripture is given by inspiration of God, and is profitable for doctrine, for reproof, for correction, for instruction in righteousness."

"Wow!" I exclaimed, "I need this. I need to read the Word of God!"

It was then I realized I had heard from the Lord. The guys in white coats were not going to come, and so far, there was not a bolt of lightning in sight. In my lonely desperation He had met my need and comforted me.

I bought a Bible and began to read every day for hours. Steve was not yet a believer and was a little jealous of my newfound passion. He thought it would wreck our marriage.

I was so excited every time I read something new (and it was all new) that I wanted to share it with him. He didn't want to hear it. But I still read. I read and read and read. I was starving for the Word of God in my life. I couldn't wait for the children to be tucked in so I could read my Bible.

By the grace of God, Steve came to know the Lord a few months later.

I remember talking with a friend, and every time we would talk our discussion would turn into a Bible study. Oh, how hungry I was! I remember telling her, "Reading the Bible is like Chinese food. You think you get your fill, but then a couple of hours later, you want some more."

I don't know when I stopped hungering for God's word on a regular basis. My hunger pains were no longer recognizable. If someone began a conversation with me about the Word of God, I would again get excited, but I didn't stay that way for long. I was like a person who had gone on a starvation diet. Food just wasn't that big of a deal anymore.

Oh, how the Lord must have grieved when I stopped reading His Word.

I actually found myself handling my Bible a little rougher so it would have that "used" look. I rarely had to search for my Bible on Sunday mornings because it would still be in the van from the Sunday before.

I had the desire to be in God's Word, but I also had my excuses. *I have too many responsibilities*, I would remind myself. *I can't get up early because someone always gets up with me. I just don't have the time.*

Then I made the decision that I would not read anything else in the morning (not even a cereal box) before I read my Bible. Well, that worked for a time, but I was only reading the Word out of obedience. I was not hungering for His Word. I wanted to once again feel the passion of that first love.

As I continued to seek the Lord, He began to show me how I had ignored the hunger pains. At the top of my list was cleaning the house, using the computer, eating meals, and a variety of other chores that a mother of eight children must get done each day. The Bible just naturally sank to the bottom of my priority list. Everything in my life reflected that the Bible was at the bottom of the list, and that everything else was more important. I had ignored my hunger for His Word for so long I no longer even noticed that I was hungry.

I wanted to impart to my children a passion for God and for His Word. But it struck me that if I couldn't even make God's Word a priority in my life, why would my children?

One morning as I was holding my Bible in my hand preparing to read it out of obedience, I felt an old familiar stirring deep within my spirit. The only emotion I can really compare it to is how I used to feel when I would see Steve on the Air Force Base in his uniform. Because he was an officer and I was enlisted, I couldn't just run up to him and kiss him, or hug him, or even acknowledge that we knew each other. I would have to wait until he came home that evening. When I heard his car pull into the garage, I would feel a stirring within me. My heart told me I could never live without this man in my life.

As I held my Bible in my hand, it felt so good. I was starting to feel hunger pains deep in my spirit once again. Just as I realized long ago that I never wanted to live without Steve, I was starting to wonder how I had lived without a daily dose of the Word for so long. I did not want to live without it any more. I could not live without it!

As my passion for the Word was renewed, I wanted to share my passion with my children. I desperately desired to impart the truth of God's Word to them. I wanted them to know that the Bible that I held in my hand gives them life. The God who breathed those words is the very same God who breathed life into them and into me and into all the world. He is the God who created the universe and all that is within it. He is the same God who sits on the throne in heaven. He is the same God to whom we can cry out "Abba Father." He is the Father who allows us to come and sit at His feet. He is the Father who gave up His only son to die on a cross for us.

My children must know my passion for God. If they do not, I have failed in the very directive that I have been given by God. I want to live out Deuteronomy 6:5 that says, "You shall love the LORD your God with all your heart, with all your soul, and with all your strength." That is passion, my friends. "And these words which I command you today shall be in your heart. You shall teach them diligently to your children, and shall talk of them when you sit in your house, when you walk by the way, when you lie down, and when you rise up" (Deuteronomy 6:6-7). Read the rest of Deuteronomy 6. It's powerful stuff!

When God reveals to us a truth, He doesn't just tell us once. He continues to reinforce it. Remember Job. In all his trials where did his strength lie? He said, "I have not departed from the commandment of His lips; I have treasured the words of His mouth more than my necessary food" (Job 23:12).

When Jesus was tempted by the devil, where did He find His strength? "But He answered and said, 'It is written, Man shall not live by bread alone, but by every word that proceeds from the mouth of God'" (Matthew 4:4, see also Deuteronomy 8:3).

If you find that you have lost your fervency and love for God, begin to seek His face. As you continue to seek Him, you will find Him. Remember His promise, "And you will seek Me and find Me, when you search for Me with all your heart" (Jeremiah 29:13). As you enter into His presence and worship at His feet, there you will find life, love, and intimacy with your Creator.

Ask God to give you a hunger for His Word that makes the Scriptures more important to you than your daily bread. If you have been starving, begin to gorge yourself with His Word. It will bring you back to life. If you have been crying out, "Lord, where are You?" He can be found within the pages of His Book. Read it! Devour it! Meditate upon it! Live it!

If you have not yet read your Bible today, begin right now. You have no excuse. You are obviously not busy because you are reading this book. If you don't know where to start, may I suggest Deuteronomy 6. I bet you won't be able to stop there.

20

GET GOD

A PAIN ENDURED

In the midst of pain that seems unbearable,
where can I find relief?
When the world ceases to offer me amazement
and wonder,
where can I go to be awed?
When the weight of my load forces me to the
ground,
where can I go to be picked up?
When tears stop flowing because they have run
dry,

where can I go to find refreshment?
When my head aches and my heart is heavy,
where can I go to dull the pain?

Anguish overcomes me!
I have no place to turn.
I try to run, to flee, to leave what causes the
    pain,
but alas, it is to no avail.
The pain follows, even intensifies, as I am pur-
    sued by the memory.
I close my eyes—
perhaps it will help if I cannot see…
But the pain is deep!

Thoughts of a better life, a richer life, envelop me.
I begin to fantasize as I journey to a land far
    away.
Then a car honks outside my window,
and I am brought back to the here and the now.

I cry out!
Again the tears come,
the tears I thought had dried up so long ago.
I beg for God to come quickly.
The pain is too much to bear.

Yesterday I was walking down easy street,
and today, it is different.
Will I prevail?

Will I stand firm in my faith?
Or will I falter and give Satan a foothold in my
    door.
"Please, Lord!" I cry. "End my pain!"
But the pain remains.

As I plea for the pain to end,
I beg God to cradle me.
"Take me in Your arms, Father.
Rock me.
I need Your unconditional love."

Then I look to the cross.
I see the pain on Your face.
I see Your nail scars and the blood.
It is at that moment
I can lift my head out of the mire that has
    engulfed me.
I can lift up my head and say,
"*You* loved me!
You love me!"
I see Your outstretched arms,
broken and beaten,
willing to wrap me up in them.

You model for me all that I am to be.
You show me that "man" will hurt me.
"Man" will cause me pain.
But You never will.
You will be there—always.

But...I must forgive!
Just as You have forgiven me
for all that I have done.
Healing will not come,
until I can forgive.
I want to hold on to the pain.
I don't want to forgive.
But I trust You know the best way.

As I bow down,
on my knees,
at Your feet,
You help me to forgive.
You help me to see that forgiveness is only for
     me.
Its healing power is only for me to feel and for
     me to see.

Oh how I want to stay here at Your feet!
Must I go on?
Must I return to the people who have hurt me so?
Must I return to a life that now seems overcome
     with pain?

Yes, I must go on.
But I do not go on alone.
You are there at my side,
giving me relief.
You are my *awesome* God.
You pick me up
and refresh my soul.

I can still feel the pain,
but You have enveloped it in Your love.
I must bear the pain,
but it is buffered by You.
You're like a giant aspirin for my soul.

I can move on from this moment and go forth
to the victory in my life that awaits me.
But I still feel hesitant.
What if You walk away from me?
But Your word says *never* will You leave or for-
    sake me.
I take comfort in those words.

I leave my prayer closet
as You wipe away my tears.
Moments ago, I didn't know how I could go on,
and now I'm preparing to fix dinner for my
    family.

Then my little daughter comes to me.
"Mommy, look, a flower!"
And again, I am awed by Your creation.
And the small child who knows not the word
    "weed."

To all people pain will come. It's what we do
with that pain that counts.

We have choices. We can hide our pain under a
rug, get angry, get debilitated, get even (that used to
be my personal favorite), get scared, or Get God!

I choose to Get God! I don't always get Him right away, however. Sometimes I go through the first five steps before I Get God. Hopefully, in my aged wisdom (I say that with a great deal of rip-roaring laughter), I am learning to Get God first.

He has shown me that He never fails. He has shown me that His will for my life is perfect and that even though I must pass through some fires, He is in charge of the heat.

I still drift into the mindset that for me life *should* always be smooth and easy. That is when I *need* His refinement. If I'm just sitting back on my haunches without need of God, I am in *big* trouble.

If I'm not needing Him in my life, that tells me that I am not doing much that is worthy to advance His kingdom. I don't believe we should sit around waiting for the next trial to come into our lives. But I also don't think we should sit around and think we are immune from trials and pain. No immunization exists for trials.

We are to be prepared for whatever may come our way. When trials that may threaten the very fiber upon which our lives rest come to us, we need to be prepared to deal with them properly. How do we get prepared? We practice by going to God daily, by calling on Him to do battle for us whether the problems seem great or small.

At my church we sing a song called, "The Battle Belongs to the Lord." I often wonder, *How many of us go into battle thinking we're the "General"?*

I'm reminded that the Lord is in charge when we sing, "When the powers of darkness come in like a flood, the battle belongs to the Lord." When life is dark, we must get the Light!

How many times does something difficult happen, and we first call on a friend, a pastor, or a church leader, or mom, before we Get God?

We need to be fit for battle. If we haven't exercised (prayed), we aren't ready for battle. The battle will continue to rage around us as we try to fight in our own strength.

When it comes to prayer, God is not some giant cosmic slot machine that when we put in our request out pops what we want. Throughout our lives (short as they are) we will be in battle. At times He may place us on the "front lines" of the battle. While on the front lines, He may allow us to take bullets. He may even allow us to die.

You may think your side is losing. You may think that it's a lost cause. But just remember that no matter how the battle is going, God is on your side. Do not give up on Him because He will not give up on you.

Remember those two simple words as you go about this thing called "life"—Get God!

GET GOD!

Get Him when you rise up.
Get Him when things are going well.
Get Him when you feel troubled.

Get Him instead of your mom.
Get Him when you cannot go on.
Get Him because He gave Himself for you.
Get God—first!

FIRST AID

If I love the Lord as much as I say I do, shouldn't I be on street corners witnessing to the lost? Shouldn't I be telling everyone I meet about the marvelous love of Jesus? Shouldn't I be inviting the lost, the widows, and the orphans to live in my home?

Is staying home with my children, home schooling them, preparing meals for them, vacuuming, dusting (okay, skip the dusting), washing clothes, cleaning floors, bathing babies enough? Or is there more that I should be doing to further the gospel of Christ?

One day as I was doing some soul searching, the Lord brought to mind some of the people who had made the greatest impact on my life. He reminded me that the *real* influences on my life were those "behind the scenes" people. They were the people in my life who administered "first aid." They were the ones who got me through the rough times. They were the ones who brought me closer to a saving knowledge of Jesus Christ. They were the unsung heroes who saved my life!

I recalled a boy in my ninth grade English class who witnessed to me. It was the first time someone actually told me that I needed to accept Jesus into my life. I could not even remember the boy's name, but I remembered His Savior's name. That faithful, young servant planted a seed and brought me closer to saying "Yes!" to Jesus. I wonder if after talking with me at school, did he go home and pray for me?

Then, He reminded me of my high school English teacher. After I graduated from high school she continued to pray frequently for me. At the time, I didn't even know she was praying for me. I returned home, on leave from the Air Force, and went to see her. How her heart must have broken to see that I was not living a godly lifestyle, that I was turning away from my parents, that I was going down a path that was headed for destruction. On that day I poured out my heart to her, she administered first aid. Did she pray for me many years after that? I believe she did.

My aunt and uncle also interceded on my behalf. They never ceased to lift me up in prayer. They never thought I was a hopeless case; though I myself did. They never gave up on me. They continued giving me first aid.

There was the wife of my husband's co-worker. She too gave me first aid. There were the people at the small Bible church that I began attending with my young children. They also administered first aid.

I have often wondered how many more "behind the scenes" people administered first aid to me so that I could live!

These heroes in my life are the people who, prompted by the Holy Spirit, got down on their knees and prayed for me. They are the ones who saved my life!

It wasn't the person out on the street evangelizing, or the pastor of a church, or the missionaries in Mozambique. It was the prayers of the saints.

I wonder if someone prayed for a hedge of protection to surround me as I walked around that Los Angeles neighborhood at night, alone, a young, naive girl from Iowa who was living in the "big city" for the first time. Was I protected because someone was praying for me?

As I sat on the side of the freeway at 4:00 in the morning beside my broken-down car, were prayers going up on my behalf?

Did someone pray when the unspeakable happened? Did someone pray that I could forgive and heal?

When I was lost, alone, and frightened did someone get down on his knees?

When I felt there was no point in living, did someone cry out for me?

When the invitation to receive salvation was given, was there one person who knew how hard it was for me to raise my hand? Was there one person who prayed with all her might that I would come? Was there one?

Many years have come and gone. I wonder how many times people have prayed for me?

When I lay in a pool of blood on the floor of my bathroom, was there one?

As my son struggled for life, was there one? Was there one who was called from his sleep to pray? Was there one who got on his knees and began to reach out to the Father, to appeal to Him on my behalf, on behalf of my son, on behalf of my seven children and their daddy? Was there one who administered first aid?

Yes! And our precious Savior heard each and every one of those prayers. And He said, "Live!"

As we struggle, wondering if what we are doing is all we can do for Christ, I say, "No!" But, you do not have to quit home schooling, or being a stay-at-home mom so you can start witnessing on street corners.

Dear women, all you have to do is become a volunteer in the Lord's Royal Red Cross. You don't have to join the Army. Administer first aid to a lost and dying world. Be the *one*!

If it hadn't been for those people who were willing to take their orders from the "General," where would we all be?

How desperately I want to be a woman of prayer! I want to be the one who calls on the Father and a life is saved. I want to be the one who cries out and a broken family is put back together. I want to be the one who sees lives changed for God. I want to be the one who never gives up on someone—the person who keeps on praying, even when it looks like all hope is gone. I want to be the old persistent woman detaining the Judge at His door.

We are in a unique position as home schooling moms. We can stop whatever we are doing to get down on our knees to pray. There is no chance that we will get fired from our job for "public display of religion." Enter the Holy of Holies and plead for those around you who have been injured by the enemy.

When God says, "Pray!" be the one who says, "Yes, Lord."

Chapter

22

To Die For!

I was in my room pouting—suffering tremendously from another bout of PPMS (Poor, Pitiful Me Syndrome)—when my thoughts automatically turned into a conversation with God: "Lord, I never get to do anything I want. I mean, thank You for these children, Lord, and for entrusting them to me. I know they are only on loan from You, but…"

That's when I was going to start complaining about never getting to do what *I* wanted to do. "I can't even sleep all night if I want to. I can't even get sick like other people." I had a *long* list in my head that I wanted to "share" with the Lord.

But, before I could begin sharing my list of complaints, I was interrupted. In my spirit I heard the phrase, "To die for." I guess that would be called praying in the Spirit because I was only focused on complaining—not on dying.

I began to ponder the phrase over and over. *To die for...to die for...* My mind raced as I tried to figure out its meaning. I thought about a commercial I had seen about some product and a teenage girl who said it was "to die for." I couldn't even remember the name of the product, but I did remember thinking "to die for" was a ridiculous term to use. It seemed to cheapen what the Lord did for us on the cross.

As I sought the Lord and asked Him what He was trying to tell me, my eyes welled up with tears. My prayer of complaint turned into a prayer of repentance. I started realizing that most of the problems I have in my home are because of my own selfishness.

I decided right then and there that if the phrase "to die for" came into my head, I was to drop whatever I was doing and tend to the need at hand. That meant I could not ask someone else to do the job—I was to do it myself.

I began living my life as usual. A few nights later I was reaching a state of hysteria as I was trying to get dinner on the table. Steve was busy. Ashley was reading. Christi was entertaining the smaller children in the basement, and Erica was screaming. I knew she just wanted to be held by someone.

I yelled, "Ashley, come hold Erica!"

Then I heard … "To die for."

"What does that mean now, Lord? Am I supposed to cease cooking dinner right when it is almost done? Am I supposed to let Erica cry? Am I supposed to let Ashley continue reading?"

A calmness swept over me in spite of the circumstances. Usually a screaming baby at dinnertime frazzles my nerves. But I was calm.

What is this? I thought. I picked up Erica, not out of frustration, but with an overwhelming sense of love for her.

"I can meet your need, Erica. I can hold you, love you, kiss you, and dinner is almost done."

We danced through the kitchen together as I checked pans for progress. I turned off the oven and set the table (not *my* job). I skipped the tablecloth— it was just too hard to toss it on the table with Erica sitting precariously on my hip. She wasn't able to hold on by herself, so I had to keep a bit of a grip on her.

In a couple of minutes, I was able to call everyone for dinner in a calm voice. For a fleeting moment my mind went to the familiar, "I slaved over this food, and now I'm not even going to get to eat it because Erica wants to eat." Then I heard again… "To die for."

Yes, I would die for her, I thought. *I would die for everyone in this house. What's the big deal about eating food that is a little cooler?*

"To die for" has changed the tone of our house. What am I willing to do for my family? Am I willing to do what it takes for my husband to trust me? Am I willing to stop what I'm doing to fix a broken toy, or find a lost "lovey"? What about getting up really early—like before 7:30 A.M. to fix a nice, warm breakfast? (Okay, God isn't finished with me yet!)

So much of our current culture is about serving self. I always *thought* I was serving my family, but I had a slave mentality! I was not serving out of a sense of love but out of a sense of duty.

I am now trying to have a "to die for" mentality. "To die for" is more than doing good deeds or being extra nice. It's lowering your standards in cleanliness so your children can learn how to do jobs around the house. It's allowing a few crumbs around the edges to have a younger child "help" with the vacuuming. It's about taking a child who has been sulky all day for a nice walk with Mom. It's bringing out the Play-Doh even if company is coming in an hour (Okay, that's stretching it a bit far, but I think you get the idea).

We all tend to want things done *our* way, and in *our* time. Having an attitude of "to die for" is crucifying our own wants, our own needs, and our own desires for the greater good of all in our household.

I look forward to bedtime because that is when I finally get to have "my" time. After we worship and pray together as a family, I am off-duty. Steve takes over getting all the children tucked in while I sit— and I usually just sit—until he comes back down.

One particular night there were more things than usual that needed to be done. I was pretty tired and had been looking forward to being off-duty. Then someone called down that David didn't have sheets on his bed. They were still in the dryer. I made a bit of a growling noise in my throat as I moaned to myself, *I want to sit, not put sheets on someone's bed!* I was going to do it, of course, but then… "To die for."

But I'm doing it, I reasoned to myself.

Then I heard the still small voice, "But not with a 'to die for' attitude."

Immediately the Lord gave me strength to get up out of my chair to go "die for" my son who needed a good night's sleep on some clean sheets.

Five minutes later I was settled back in my chair. Eventually Steve joined me after he had finished his nightly duty of kissing all of the kids goodnight. As he walked in the room, he looked at me with a strange look. (You know how your husband stares at you sometimes like you have a big blob of mustard on your nose?)

"What?" I said, as I instinctively reached up and rubbed my nose.

"You look different," he said.

I furrowed my brow at him.

"You look…really happy!"

Set your minds on things above, not on earthly things. For you died, and your life is now hidden with Christ in God. When Christ, who is your life, appears, then you also will appear with Him in glory. (Colossians 3:2-4 NIV)

Chapter
25

BRYAN'S
SONG

As I lay in bed, I instinctively, lovingly, rested my hand on my pregnant belly. Little did I know as I felt the kicking of my unborn baby that in just a few short minutes my life would be changed forever.

The time was getting nearer for our eighth baby to be born. I had been having contractions all day. I figured our baby would be born that night or the next day when I went to my scheduled appointment.

I crawled out of bed to go use the bathroom— again. Anyone who has ever been pregnant knows that this is a ritual done virtually every night in the latter stages of pregnancy. Go to the bathroom, go to bed, wait ten minutes, get up again to use the bathroom, and the cycle continues until you finally fall asleep.

As I sat on the toilet, I began to get excited because I thought my water had broken. But the flow didn't stop. And I began feeling chunks coming out. I called for Steve to come in and turn on the light.

My fears were confirmed. I had been filling the toilet with blood. As Steve ran to get the phone to call 9-1-1, I fell onto the floor.

I knew at that moment, I was probably going to die. I even told Steve I was going to die. I was not fearful, just matter of fact. I don't remember thinking about our children at that point, but I did not want to leave Steve.

I wish I could say it was like the movies where the world stands still for a moment as a man cradles his wife's body in his arms as she whispers her final words, "I love you" to him.

But this was not anything like the movies. There were arrangements that had to be made. Steve called a sitter to come stay with the children, and then he called my sister to pray.

By now the ambulance had arrived. The paramedics gave me oxygen, put an IV in my arm, and began pumping fluids through my veins. I began to feel better, but I was still pretty sure I was not going to make it. I was not frightened. In fact, I really felt quite peaceful.

A second ambulance came. The intention was to load me up, meet another ambulance, and switch me to it; however, the third ambulance was only six miles away, so we waited for it.

The big dilemma was how to get me down the stairs. Do paramedics only deal with people on ground floors? Their biggest fear was that I was going to deliver the baby. At one point, one of the ambulance crew put the pulse monitor on my finger.

"Ow!" I groaned.

The paramedic got a little panicky and asked, "Are you having the baby?"

"No, you pinched my finger." We all chuckled.

I was worried my children would wake up, but none of them stirred from their rooms, so I assumed all the children were asleep. Little did I know, Ashley was wide-awake in her room. She knew that was the best place for her to stay. She watched from her window as I was placed into the back of the ambulance. She even took a picture of the ambulances in the driveway. She thought it was the last time she might ever see me. After we were gone, Ashley came out of her room and prayed with the sitter.

The ambulance ride seemed really fast. If I weren't in the back, I would have thought it quite exciting to see three ambulances whizzing past with lights and sirens. Steve rode up front and prayed even more intensely when the attendant with me in the back told the driver, "Floor it!"

I was freezing. I couldn't stop my teeth from chattering. My blood pressure was dangerously low at fifty-eight over thirty-two.

Upon arriving at the hospital, I was greeted by more people than I could remember. Some guy started doing an ultrasound. They seemed unconcerned that my baby was going to die if they didn't take it out.

But I was still peaceful. I later found out that I was in shock and taking me into the operating room at that time would have had dire consequences. After three ultrasounds, they finally prepped me for surgery.

Once in the operating room, I only remember a calmness. I felt like someone was praying for me. It was really quite a pleasant feeling. At one point I asked if anyone noticed from the ultrasound the sex of my baby.

Only the anesthesiologist responded. He kindly leaned over to me and said, "We weren't looking." I just wanted to know what sex my baby would be when I arrived in heaven with it.

Steve waited in the hallway while the surgery took place. As he watched through the window and could see only doctors, nurses, and a whole lot of blood, he felt an unusual peace, too. He was uncomfortable feeling so peaceful. He was sitting in a chair at the end of the hallway and would begin to think, *I should be worried.* Then he would start to worry. He would get up, walk to the operating room window, look in, and even with a view of lots of blood, he would again become peaceful. He could feel God's presence with him.

The next thing I knew, several hours had passed. When I awoke, someone told me I had a boy. The doctors were worried the baby had inhaled blood into his lungs, so they were sending him to a children's hospital an hour and a half away. A nurse wheeled the baby into my room. He had a ventilator tube in his mouth and a tube sticking out of his belly button. The doctor had sent a scope of some kind up through his umbilical cord to his heart.

As I looked at him I thought, *That isn't really my baby.*

His fate was still unknown. The doctor said the baby probably had massive brain damage. The outlook for him was bleak, but I still had an incredible peace.

Over the course of the next several days, even weeks, the pieces began to fit together. I had a condition known as *placenta accreta*. My placenta was in full praevia position, but my placenta had grown through my uterine wall and attached to several of my organs. The doctor was unable to stop the bleeding. He had to perform a hysterectomy.

At one point during the surgery, my blood pressure bottomed out and my oxygen levels dropped below 50 percent. After they pumped twelve units of "new" blood into me, my condition began to improve. When I finally came out of the anesthesia, my chances had gone from slim to much improved.

Our son also improved gradually. While he rode in the ambulance to the other hospital, they told us his breathing improved. He even opened his eyes for the first time. They were able to reduce the ventilator to 60 percent. Every report from then on was positive as God multiplied His blessings to us.

After five days I was able to go home, but home is not where I went. I went to the bedside of my son, Bryan. I had to wait an hour and a half before I could hold him. He nursed right away, and we were able to take him home the next day. It didn't appear that he had any brain damage.

I believe that the Lord had been preparing me for this almost my entire pregnancy. It was a miserable pregnancy. It was the first time I was questioning if I really wanted to go through having another baby. But in my heart, I knew I could not, in good conscience, do anything to prevent a pregnancy. Steve and I felt convicted that we should let God be in control of our family size. We knew God was the Creator of life. Children were blessings to be desired.

At one point during my pregnancy, I told the Lord in prayer that if I were not to have any more children it would have to be by His hand, not by ours. I did not know when I went to bed on Feb 11, 1998 as I lovingly touched my round belly that that would be the last time I would ever feel a baby kick within my body. I was thirty-three when Bryan, my eighth child, was born. I figured I could possibly have another eight before I was through. It is so easy to take fertility for granted.

Since that night, my life has changed dramatically. The little things don't seem to matter anymore. My children could have been without a mommy. My husband could have been without a wife. Of course, I would have been in heaven, so I probably wouldn't have cared too much.

The Lord has given me a new life. I really thought when I came home from the hospital that I would be perfect. For some reason I felt that I had almost touched the hand of God, so somehow that would make me a perfect mommy. Right away, I blew it. So, I'm not going to get to be perfect—yet! But I won't stop trying!

I'm enjoying my life more, enjoying my children more, and enjoying my husband more. So many things seem to get in the way of what is really important. I hope that I never get to a point again when I cannot marvel at God for saving the life of my son and myself. I hope that I will not forget to marvel at the blue sky, the snow-covered grass, the intoxicating smell of a newborn baby, a two-year-old singing "Jesus Wuvs Me," and the sparkle in the eyes of a child when you throw all abandon to the wind and say, "Let's have soda-pop for lunch!"

When God saved my life, He put a new beat in my heart, more spring in my step, joy in my soul, and a miracle in my arms.

In the mundane, there is *life*!

Chapter 24

JUST A MOMMY

Shortly after my brush with death, a woman I dearly respect told me, "God clearly has something more in store for you than just being a mommy to these children."

I began to think about that. *Yes*, I decided, *He does have something more in store for me*. I then began to ask God what He had in mind.

I've always wanted to change the world. I didn't have small dreams as a child—I had astronomical dreams. I was going to be the President of the United States in the year 2000. I had planned for a long time that I would be the first woman President, and I would do it the year I turned thirty-five. Thirty-five seemed so far away at the time.

Well, the year 2000 is here, and I haven't even thrown in my hat as a candidate. I guess I better give up on that one—at least this year. Maybe I should try for 2004?

After Bryan's miraculous birth and my near-death experience, I desperately felt I needed a literal "mountain." I wanted to proclaim God's glory to the world from atop a mountain. I was so excited about God's miraculous power and unfathomable love. I felt like I could climb to the top of Pike's Peak and just *yell* my story. I envisioned all the people on earth, falling down on their knees and worshiping God. Then reality took over.

I thought about what it would be like to tell my story on *Good Morning America, Oprah, The Tonight Show,* or maybe even my favorite, *Nightline. I could be the one who proves to the world that God does exist, that He cares about us, and yes, He still performs miracles in people's lives.*

I reconsidered and concluded that perhaps those shows wouldn't be interested in hearing my story. They probably wouldn't think it was that great of a miracle after all. I decided the secular talk shows were not the route I wanted to take to change the world.

I then thought the best place to proclaim the glory of God was on Focus on the Family. After this consumed my thoughts for quite awhile, I gave up on that, too.

The woman's words continued to haunt me. *God clearly has something more in store for you than just being a mommy to these children.*

I began to feel that my life had become meaningless. God had something in store for me, and I was missing it or failing to do it because of "fear" or some other problem. I began to feel an urgency about my life. I felt the need to do things, to go places, or as some might say "to get out of the boat and go for a swim."

I looked longingly at little red convertibles. At thirty-four I was already experiencing a "midlife crisis," or what I referred to as "Post-Almost-Dying Syndrome." I wanted adventure. I wanted to "go for the gusto." But every time I went somewhere, some little kid wanted to go along with me. It's really tough "going for the gusto" with a bunch of little kids in tow.

I wondered what it would be like to become a working mom. I could put all my kids in public school or day care, and go to work. Surely, I could find the "gusto" at work. There's adventure, excitement, and opportunity to change the world.

Then one night, I was up late with Bryan. Steve had gone to bed already, so I just rocked the baby in his room. Bryan looked up and smiled at me. I smiled back at him as I kissed his head. I grieved that I would never be able to have any more children. I held him in my arms for a very long time that night. He had long since fallen asleep, and I just held him. I cuddled him close and kissed his soft head. As I stared at him, he did that little sideways grin that babies do when they are sleeping.

I felt at that moment a deep yearning to be "with" my children. Holding Bryan in my arms, rocking him to sleep is exactly where God intended me to be. In that quiet moment God was using Bryan, a tiny little baby, to change me.

No, I'm not a missionary preaching the gospel to all the nations. No, I'm not proclaiming the glory of God from the mountaintops. No, my life is not filled with incredible adventures (although I do think a house full of children with the stomach flu is quite an adventure).

But…who knows, I just might be training another Mother Teresa or a Billy Sunday or a future doctor, statesman, or mechanic who loves the Lord.

For me, there is no longer such a phrase in my mind as *just a mommy* to these children. These children are my "gusto!"

Conclusion

A Moment in Time

Have you ever had a "moment" in time when suddenly your life changed forever? If you have been alive for long, you have probably experienced some monumental moments like your wedding, the birth of your first baby, a move to a new city, a new job, or the moment you found Jesus and asked Him to be your Savior.

But sometimes a life changing moment happens unexpectedly. One day as you're minding your own business—Whammo! —you listen to a tape, get convicted, and now you're a home schooling mom. Or maybe you're unhappy at home, tired of the mundane tasks that go along with raising your children, and suddenly God calls you to be The Greatest Mom Ever. You have a renewed sense of purpose in this task of mother, mentor, diaper-dipper, and face-washer.

There are times when those moments are horrible—the fire that destroyed your home, the heart attack that killed your dad, the baby that died before he ever saw your face. Those Tear Moments are the hardest to bear. Depending on how we face those moments, we either become stronger or weaker in our faith. We either learn to lean on God more, or we pull away and try to make sense of it all alone, on our own terms. Often in our loneliness and pain, we embrace bitterness over grace.

I'll never forget reading *Abe Lincoln Grows Up* by Carl Sandburg. When Lincoln was a young boy, his mother had a little baby that died a few days after his birth. Lincoln's mother was never the same after that. She lost her zest for life.

I just happened to be reading this particular part of the book while holding our dear Bryan who was two-weeks old at the time. As I looked down at my precious son, I thought to myself, *That could have been me. I could have been the one who lost her zest for life. Yet, here I am holding our son whom God miraculously gave to me.* I could not continue reading. I sat on the couch, babe in arms, and wept.

I am fascinated and amazed at how God weaves those God Moments into our lives to soften our spirits and to make us more like Him. Jesus showed us what it means to suffer and at the same time how to forgive. He made the most of every moment to show us God's grace and mercy. I try to see the moments that appear to me as bad or uncomfortable in my life, as merely a piece of the puzzle that God is completing in me.

I've often felt that moments in our lives are like pieces in a puzzle. God takes those pieces, the good and the bad, and He fits them all together to form one complete picture that tells the whole story of our lives here on earth.

Until the puzzle is done, I do not know what it will look like. My only hope is that many pieces in the puzzle will be a picture of me touching people's hearts with God's love. That is why I write. I write because just maybe God can use me to touch the life of someone else, that just maybe I can comfort someone who is isolated and hurting. Perhaps within my grasp lies the ability to add a moment to the life of someone else. This hope drives me to my knees.

I long for a glimpse into the future to see what moments will be the important ones that shape my children. What moments will be the pieces within their puzzle that mattered the most? It would be nice to be able to wipe out those moments that I wish would not have happened—like the time I blew up about spilled juice on *my* clean floor, or when I broke the pencil in my frustration over a child not "getting it" after I explained it *three* times already, or all the other ridiculous moments when I threw all my godly mothering skills out the window. I would like to be able to erase those moments, but unlike my word processor, life does not come with a delete key.

We cannot change the moments in our lives. We can only grow and learn from them. I would hope that if tragedy were to strike, I would be able to lean on Jesus to find my comfort in His loving arms. I would hope that the moment that changed my life would be a moment redeemed by God.

When I almost died the night of Bryan's birth, my children and my husband could have very easily experienced one of those moments of sorrow and of major life change.

Sometimes in a split-second life changes.

One minute your teenage son leaves the house angry, and the next minute, the police notify you that he has had a fatal accident.

One minute you talk to a loved one on the phone, and the next minute, her voice is only a memory.

One minute you are *just a mommy*, and the next you are the Greatest Mom Ever.

One minute you are in the field, and the next minute, you are meeting Jesus in the sky.

It only takes a moment for our lives to be changed forever.